You're the Boss: Make Running Work for You

A Holistic Coaching Guide for Running, Self-Development, and Self-Discovery with Practical Tools and Tips

Heinke Kauntz

Contents

Foreword

I was in California in 2010 for an exchange program when my neighbor, a regular runner, invited me to join her for an evening jog. On the spur of the moment, I agreed. Her enthusiasm was contagious and prompted me to quickly pull on my treasured Puma sneakers and fly out the door before I could change my mind or consider the suitability of my outfit. In any case, as a first-time jogger, I would not have known what would be the most comfortable outfit for the outing!

Needless to say, the outcome was two tremendous blisters on the back of my verses. Also, I did not have a sports bra, so my boobs jumped happily from one side to the other, getting almost as much exercise as my legs. To avoid certain embarrassment, I had to discreetly nudge them gently back into place a few times. But, despite the challenges, something magical was happening in my psyche—and I am not talking here about the sore muscles I felt the next day.

The memory of that evening jog, my first run so long ago, remains with me to this day. I felt free, I felt alive, and I felt an almost primitive connection between my body and nature. It is amazing how much of the environment you notice while running even a short distance. You suddenly start appreciating nature and respecting yourself for pushing through even if it is not that comfortable.

My neighbor was jogging next to me with a smile, chatting and enjoying every second, while I was busy trying not to breathe like a steam engine, not quite listening to her, and definitely not enjoying every second. *Is running only pleasant for some people?* I wondered, *or is there a way for me to make it enjoyable too?* With this question in my head, I went for another jog. This time, I convinced my roommate to join me. She was a lovely lady from Korea, but we could barely communicate as her English was very basic, and she had a thick accent. But somehow the running invitation cleared these hurdles. I waited for her in front of the house, and there she met me wearing flip-flops! Did she not understand me after all? It turned out she understood me very well as she ran the full distance in those flip-flops. I can still hardly believe it. But then again, we all start somewhere, and we all decide which path to take. There is no right or wrong; there is only doing or not doing.

Today I am running marathons and doing Ironman-distance

triathlons, and I still get blisters occasionally. Some things don't change, it seems! But I also learned so much about myself, and I truly believe that this made and is still making me a better person every day.

I am grateful that I followed my instincts that evening, even though I could have stayed home watching TV and eating cookies. Nothing against cookies; I love them. But I would rather tell my future grandchildren about my running adventures and inspire them to live boldly. And if I can do that while sipping a hot drink with some cookies, that would be the perfect scenario for me.

I hope you too will find your way through the physical and mental challenges that lead to that marvelous and rewarding space. Never give up until you find your rhythm and create amazing stories that you can share with your friends and families. The good thing about running is that you do it for yourself, so you can decide on everything and make it work for you. Remember: You're the boss!

I am excited to share my perspective, experience, and knowledge with you and wish you an incredible running adventure.

Happy running!

Introduction

Sharing the Sheer Bliss of Running

"I don't run to add days to my life, I run to add life to my days."

— Ronald Rook

One Friday afternoon, my friend Jeanne, a fitness fanatic, was invited by a colleague, Jack, to join him the next afternoon for a jog up the footpath leading to the top of the local mountain. I could almost hear the conversation in my mind when Jeanne was telling me this story years later. I hope you can, too.

"Jack, you know I am not a runner! I prefer going to the gym and working out on the elliptical, the treadmill, and the rowing machines. The gym is air-conditioned. It's dry and safe. Why on earth would I want to run up a scraggly mountain path? After a good workout, I also do some weight training, and then I hit the showers and then the juice bar. It's all very well planned and civilized," said Jeanne. "And besides, what if I twist an ankle on the mountain path? Will you piggyback me down the mountain?"

"Aw, Jeanne, you do the same things over and over again in the gym. Where is your sense of adventure?" Jack asked her.

"Seriously Jack, are you calling running up a mountain an adventure?" Jeanne grinned at her friend.

"Okay then, let's make a deal," he replied. "This Saturday afternoon, we run up my mountain path, and next Saturday, I will spend three grueling hours with you at the gym. Does that sound good?"

"Okay, I'm in," Jeanne agreed. "Will you pick me up at three at my house? Oh, and what should I wear?"

"Long stretch pants so that your legs don't get covered in scratches from the tall grass and bushes next to the trail, good quality trainers, and a running vest. You can pack some water or energy bars in the vest pockets, or you can put them in a small, lightweight running pack. And Jeanne, maybe stuff a light raincoat in that bag too. It tends to drizzle on the mountaintop." Jack was clearly delighted by the prospect of showing Jeanne the difference between the gym and a mountaintop.

"Anything else?" Jeanne quipped in reply with a bit of sarcasm in her voice.

Saturday Morning

Jeanne looked out her kitchen window and saw the top of the mountain bathed in sunlight as if an artist had just completed the painting for her eyes to see.

Suddenly, Jeanne was no longer irritated that she had agreed to go with Jack instead of going to the gym. She began to wonder what experiences she would encounter on this run up the footpath. She carried on with her chores, did some laundry, and fed Mister Tom, her large, black tabby. Jeanne decided she was going to show Jack that, although she always ran on smooth tracks and machines at the gym, she was quite capable of running up the mountain path.

And then the doorbell rang. It was three p.m. exactly. Jack was standing at her door with a big smile: "Come on, Jeanne! We have to hurry. I want to show you the most beautiful sunset in the world. The sun sets at seven, and the view across the lake is unbelievable at that time."

Jack parked his Range Rover at the park ranger's hut and told the ranger on duty they would be back just after sunset. Joe, the friendly ranger, seemed to know Jack quite well. He said "Hi there, I bet you forgot to bring flashlights, right? Don't worry. It happens. Here is one for each of you, and I will be here when you get back. Enjoy yourselves but be safe. Jack, the jogger's path was cleaned up and checked just two days ago, so it should be a smooth trip!"

The Majestic Mountaintop

"Well, come on then!" Jack said as they reached the path, "Let's do some stretches for our cold muscles. We don't want to pull a muscle on the mountain."

Jack's routine led them through loosening the neck muscles by moving their heads from side to side, up and down, and all the way back. Next came the arm stretches to the sky and then some more to each side, diagonally across their chests. After that, it was forward lunges and toe touches, finishing off with rotational 'angel wing' circles with their arms.

Ready, Set, Go...

They started walking at a fast pace and after about half a mile, began a slow but steady jog up the long, gradual incline.

At one point, Jeanne became aware of the sounds around them. "Hey, do you hear the birds and the squirrels and the sounds the trees and leaves are making?"

Jack grinned, "Of course I do! This is why I prefer running in the clean and clear fresh air of the mountain instead of at the gym or on a track! To me, it feels like the whole forest is alive and in harmony with nature, and I become a part of that harmony. It makes me relax and forget about work, traffic, and any other things on my mind. I concentrate on my running, the air, the sounds of the trees, and the little creatures."

"Jack, how far to go before the peak?"

"I'd say in total about three miles, and we will give it a good run where it steepens at the top. That's only half a mile, the end of a pretty good workout if you consider that we've been running at an incline and you haven't noticed," said Jack with a laugh.

"Absolutely! And you are right: I didn't look back, so I forgot that we were running on an incline. We are going to have to stretch those glutes and shins—especially me!"

They soon ran the last half a mile. Jeanne was silent, and Jack didn't want to interrupt his friend's thoughts drinking in the beauty below them for the first time. They just stood there, looking at the lake below with its border of trees and shrubs, all framed by a perfectly clear sky above, and watched as the sun gently dipped to the horizon.

Jeanne turned to Jack and said, "I feel as if I'm in another world, one where beauty, nature, and health coincide. All the stress and anxiety from work this past week are gone. I can't even recall what I stressed about. It's a kind of magic."

Jack smiled at his friend. "This is what I wanted to share with you—the sheer bliss of running. Yes, you can run at the gym or on the track, but there are times when your mind needs to relax and regenerate, and I've found that nature heals and mentally refreshes me. The pure joy of running in nature enables me to start the next stressful week from a relaxed calm state—physically and mentally."

Sharing and Caring

Jeanne and Jack were sitting on a rock drinking some water and eating their snack bars when Jack opened up to Jeanne. They had been colleagues and work friends for over a decade, but Jeanne only then realized how little she knew about Jack.

Jack said that after his divorce, he started going to the gym and found himself drawn to running, so he concentrated on that. He had been through a tough time and had noticed that although he was physically fitter than ever before, there was a part of his mind that needed more to heal from the trauma. That was when he realized that opening his fixed mindset was the change that he needed, and exercising and running on the treadmill at the gym was not enough.

Jack told Jeanne that he began to research changing from a fixed mindset to a growth mindset, which would guide him to combine other methods of dealing with past traumas with the physical benefits of exercise.

"I knew running was for me, but I knew I had to learn more about how exercise affects our minds and how we can use running to train our brains, spirits, and bodies to once again become the whole beings we were meant to be. As I started asking around, I found many people, both men, and women, who were trying to deal with trauma by running. The kind of fixed mindset that we all have doesn't change when we only exercise. We need a way to incorporate the mind and spirit to gain full healing."

He peered down at the view before continuing. "It was then that I remembered my dad brought me to the top of the mountain when he was struggling with decisions he had to make at work. I put it all together and realized that besides physical beings, we are spiritual and natural beings, and what better place to recharge your batteries than in the middle of nature? That was when I started running, although I started by just walking in the park. It's almost as if the wind, the rain, the birds, and the tiny animals carry your worries away.

"After coming up the mountain for some weeks, I felt I was a totally changed person. I felt free again. My body, my mind, and my spirit were free, and they were once again naturally connecting along the neural pathways that had always been there. These neural pathways had become slightly hidden and dormant after my trauma, but using running and mental relaxation combined with nature seemed to be the perfect way to reconnect the tracks. Soon I was back to my old happy self again, and the trauma of the past years was forgotten. I had found an amazing new way to exercise that helped my mind repair the hurt it had been through.

He paused and smiled. 'I wanted you to experience this

firsthand so that you can see and feel the change that has already begun inside you after only one visit to this spot at the top of the world where you can see everything beneath you and know how brave you are just to face daily life. From here, you are looking at the world below like a giant from his castle. When you look at the scale of the world below, you will see there is nothing to fear, and you are able to overcome any of life's obstacles.

"Jeanne, this is not all hocus-pocus from my clever brain alone. There's a book that I found that set me on this path and that I am going to introduce you to. It will give you tips and tricks for every situation—physical, mental, and spiritual—that will help you to grow into the confident woman you should be. Let me give you some glimpses into what you will learn without a 'spoiler alert.' I know I'm sounding like a college professor, but believe me, your life is going to change more than it ever did in college."

Begin with these tips on your journey of discovery and the adventure of your life:

- Discover and define your personal *inspiring goals* and the tools and tricks you will need to achieve them.
- Learn how to stay *motivated* and become your own biggest cheerleader, even when the going gets tough.
- Set yourself up for *success*, then *enjoy* the ride and *celebrate* like crazy.
- In the process, you will be writing down achievable, realistic goals.
- Follow this up by determining *how* you are going to achieve each goal and then set a target date for when it must be completed.
- In perhaps the most important and inspiring act of all, write down (for your eyes only) what the catalyst was that made you realize you needed help to move forward into living your best life—growing instead of just existing. You can revisit this every time your motivation flags.

This book is comprehensive and includes 'cheat sheets' that you can carry in your bag for those days when you are feeling low. In addition, you can trust the advice in this book because the author spent years researching the subject matter, including the interconnectedness of the mind, body, and spirit. She is a topmost aficionado.

This book is filled with the latest scientific breakthroughs to help people attain a happy, healthy, and holistic life. Unique tips are revealed throughout the book, which will allow you to mentally process them one by one rather than having to try to absorb them all in the first chapter without proper explanations and examples.

In a Nutshell...

Jack concluded: "My friend, I know you didn't want to come running up this mountain when you could have been in a well-equipped gym. But now that your lungs have breathed the cleanest air and you've seen nature from the top of the mountain, can you already imagine leading a new, better, healthier, and more balanced life, just like I'm experiencing?"

Jeanne had to agree, and so her journey of fitness changed into a journey of joyful living.

Breaking Open the Nutshell

In this book, we are going to explore everything that is needed for you to reach the innermost, tasty well-guarded delicious nut center. The essence of this book is to crack open the nut and expose the contents. This is going to show you how to take your fixed mindset and turn it into a growth mindset. In doing this, you will expose your true potential, your inner core, and automatically release your innermost desires and goals.

Marathon runners follow a rigorous training program before a major marathon. Their glutes hurt, the soles of their feet burn, and there are days when they wonder if they should give it all up. For a true marathon runner, the goal is not only to excel in the physical aspects of running but to build the strength and mental resolve to push on and push through the challenges.

The True Wisdom of Running

Ancient Ancestors

Human history shows us that being a long-distance runner is part of our natural evolution. Our ancient ancestors had to chase their prey over vast distances and for many hours before they caught up to it and could add it to their daily meal. Human beings are among the slowest animals on earth, so how is it that we managed to catch our prey? It's simple really. We built up stamina after days and weeks of running, waiting for our prey to get tired. When this goal was achieved, humans could catch their prey.

Is Training a Solo Act?

Psychologists have found that people who run with a friend or in groups are generally less anxious and less depressed. This bodes well for people who want to naturally boost their serotonin, dopamine, and endorphin levels. Training for a major race takes weeks of planning when your mind is engaged in the process of planning and practicing instead of stressing when you get home from a hectic day at work. If you prefer your own company after a stressful day, running can also fit into your stress-less workout. Take a run in a quiet environment, perhaps a park near your home or, if you are lucky, along the beach.

Technique

Once you declare that running is your preferred method of exercise, you can start to focus on your technique. Before that moment, chances are that you didn't give a thought to how long your strides were, where your waist was positioned in relation to your hips, or whether you were smiling during your run. Yes, smiling! Smiling while you run makes you a more efficient runner and can build your stamina. Scientists and psychologists have determined that smiling while running is beneficial to athletes and noncompetitive runners alike.

No Pain, No Gain

If there is one adage not to learn, it is 'no pain, no gain.' If you are training correctly and stretching your muscles before and after your run, you should not have pain. Just like a racehorse in training, warm up and cool down your muscles. Plan your stretches, and incorporate them into your routine. Your pre-run and post-run workouts will be different, so figure out a routine that will suit you.

Running Gear: Fashion or Function?

While running may be your exercise of choice, the choice of what you wear is partly function and partly fashion. You will naturally have to ensure that you have the appropriate running shoes. Always buy your training shoes from a running store. They can advise you on your gait, and you can ask a professional about the 'slippage factor.'

In addition to your shoes, there are miracle fabrics that activewear is made from for the comfort of runners. All you need to know is that the shirt, windbreaker, shorts, and/or tights must suit the weather conditions and must be comfortable.

Also, give some thought to your visibility when you are running after dark. You must be able to see where you are going (so carry a flashlight or wear a headlamp), and others need to be able to see you (so wear bright, reflective apparel).

Food is Fuel

Seasoned athletes pay attention to their diet not only for health reasons but also to monitor the amount of fuel it gives their bodies. For some, the pre-marathon and post-marathon meal is pasta. Some runners prefer a big post-race meal after any long-distance run but only a small snack before short runs and a heavier breakfast after short runs. Listen to what others say about meal choices, but it's your body and your choice. Food affects both your mental and physical health, so you can rest easy and choose what works for you. You're the *boss!*

Music, Mantras, and Mental Games

Here again, it's your choice. If you can run for two hours on a 'little bit of country' or a 'little bit of rock and roll', then do it. Some people say that listening to music while trying to build their running stamina drives them nuts. If that's you, just don't do it.

As a serious runner, start incorporating visualization techniques. See and feel yourself breaking that ribbon after 26.2 miles. This is not gobbledygook, but the laws of attraction might feature in your belief system—or it might not. The choice is ultimately yours to make!

Chapter 1
Setting the Right Goals

“The trouble with not having goals is that you can spend your life running up and down the field and never score.” —
Bill Copeland

On Your Marks, Ready, Go!

Now that you have decided that running is something you would like to do, this book is here to ignite your engine and put you on the path to achieving your goal.

The principles described in this book apply to any goal that you choose. Although the book focuses on marathon running, you can adapt the principles and framework to suit your particular needs for running of any kind.

Five W's and an H

If you want to achieve success in any area of your life, even a project at work, asking certain questions will ensure you don't miss a thing.

Answering the five W's and the H question are essential in gathering information for problem-solving and planning. This method of information gathering is used by police investigators, journalists, researchers, and successful business entrepreneurs. The order in which you ask the questions will, of course, vary and can be adapted according to the situation where it is applied.

Why
Who
What
When
Where
How

Define Your *Why*

We often set goals based on other people's expectations of us. Perhaps your mother or father wanted to run marathons but could not do that due to other commitments such as work and family. Now that you are showing an interest in long-distance running, they may subconsciously be reaching for what was once their goal through you.

This process of defining your *why* is an important step and will lead you down the road to achieving your goal. If you set your goals based on other people's expectations or dreams, this might lead to not achieving your goal because it is, in fact, not your goal.

Drill down your *why* to its very core. For example, you might think, *I want to run a marathon to challenge myself.* But *why* do you want to challenge yourself? *I want to challenge myself so I can reach higher and be more confident because I followed through on the challenge. Why* do you want to do that? *I want to be confident so that I can be a better role model for my kids.* And *why* is that? *I want my kids to follow through on their dreams!*

Who—You think this Answer is Easy? Wrong!

Now that you realize that goals are sometimes affected by other people's expectations, it is time to ask yourself *who* you are setting a specific goal for. Are you setting it to please or impress someone else? Are you setting it to make a point? Or are you setting it because it is what *you* want?

If, after doing some serious soul-searching, the answer to the question of *who* is *you,* you are on the way to achieving your goal.

What **is the Goal?**

Yes, you have decided to become a marathon runner, but there is more to it than meets the eye. Have you drilled down to the core?

Is it that you want to run marathons on weekends for fun and fitness and to claim a medal from each marathon you complete, or is it more than that? Are you going to run competitively or to support causes?

Are half-marathons more your forte? Are you going for gold?

Goals require commitment and effort, so only if you have a strong enough *why*, and the commitment of the *who* is from you, can you set the goals to plan the *how*.

When **are you Going to Compete?**

Is marathon running going to be a one-time 'bucket list' venture, or do you want to make it the focal point of your life? Is marathon running going to give you the time you want to spend with your family? Are you going to include them and make marathons part of your family's healthy lifestyle?

Have you thought about marathon running as a way to expand your group of friends and meet people while getting fit and healthy?

Marathon running is exciting and energizing. Once you have felt the massive surge of adrenaline that envelops you during the process of getting ready, getting your number, and lining up for the start, it is a feeling that you will want to repeat again and again.

Where—Road or Trail?

There are so many marathons! Some city races, like the Boston Marathon, are more than a century old. Boston was first run in 1897 and is the world's oldest and most prestigious marathon.

If you dream of running in the United States of America, all marathons can be found in online calendars that will help you plan your travels and training. Or are you up for more unique and adventurous marathons, such as those in the Caribbean Islands, on the Great Wall, or in Antarctica?

Trail (also known as cross-country) marathons are very different than road marathons. In trail marathons, you run across natural terrain such as dirt and grass while paved roads are kept to a minimum. There are thousands of marathons of both types, which give you more than enough marathons to keep you busy. Have fun with this! You can choose to run the same marathons annually and make it your goal to improve your time each year, or you can run a different marathon each year. Either way, enjoy the experiences and challenges!

How? Now that's the exciting part!

This is where you will get down to the nitty-gritty of marathon training and racing. You will learn to devise a training plan for each marathon. And you will learn to set up the ultimate runner's toolbox.

If you have been a couch potato, the *how* of turning into a marathon runner is going to take a commitment from you of six months to a year. You will learn the basics and how to avoid pitfalls and rookie mistakes that can send your dream up in smoke.

Let's not forget the all-important eating plan that brings the focus on healthy eating in line with your new healthy and fit lifestyle. Hey, but don't sweat the small stuff! This is where you will get all the information you need: how to eat during your training months, your pre-marathon meal, and your post-marathon recovery meal.

Wow! This is going to be fun, and we are going to do it together. In fact, tack on some running colleagues or friends and make this a joyful group initiative.

Goal Setting

"The man who moves a mountain begins by carrying away small stones... It does not matter how slowly you go so long as you do not stop."

— Confucius

Bestselling author James Clear explains the concept of goal setting in a manner that can be adapted to your unique needs.

Start off by having the right idea about goal setting—what is it, and why is it important?

You might not be conscious of it, but we set goals every day. We have goals to achieve at work, we have goals for our family and social life, and we have goals for our health.

Society requires that we live in a goal-driven world, and once we have reached our first milestone, we must continue to run to the next milestone. However, the knowledge we have about the science of achieving goals and how to do that is where guidance is needed.

When setting personal or professional goals, there are proven methods that will make achieving them as easy as 1, 2, 3...

According to experts, goal setting can be defined as the act of setting an objective or target that you wish to attain. This makes good sense, but there is more involved—defining what success looks like to you.

In specific terms, what do you want to achieve? If you are serious about your goal, you may need to approach it from a different angle. Instead of only focusing on the success you desire, you have to consider the sacrifices that will be required to achieve these goals.

James Clear once wrote, "The real challenge is not determining if you want the result but if you are willing to accept the sacrifices required to achieve your goal."

Are you ready to accept the lifestyle changes and challenges required to reach your goal? If you have made the decision, it is time to put it into practice by following these perfect principles for success. Remember, we are all unique, and our goals must be achievable and realistic. But the time to start is now. As James Clear also stated: "Everybody wants a gold medal. Few people want to train like an Olympian."

Goals and Systems

To achieve your goal, you have to have a system in place to follow. This system should be like a manual that sets out how to get to your goal. Within this system to attain your goal will be built-in smaller goals that will bring you closer, step by step, to your main goal. For each of these smaller goals, there will be action steps that are realistic, measurable, and attainable.

As a runner, you have made it your goal to run a marathon. The system you will use to reach your goal is your training schedule.

As a coach, it is your goal to take your team to win the championship. Your system is to get your team to practice every day.

As a writer, getting your book published is your goal. Writing a certain number of words per day is the system you follow to ensure success.

If you want to make millions as a business magnate, that is your goal. Developing a successful marketing and sales strategy is your system.

The goal sets the direction; the system helps you achieve the goal. The key is knowing that these are not mutually exclusive. This will give you the winning edge.

Pitfalls of Goal Setting and How to Overcome Them

Setting and achieving your personal goals can help ensure that you lead a happy and fulfilling life that you can share with your friends, loved ones, and colleagues. We all have ambitions, as much as they may differ. Sometimes though, despite our best intentions, our goals fall by the wayside. Here are the top common pitfalls that may leave them behind in your tracks!

1. Your *Why* is not Clearly Defined

Setting a precise goal, including step-by-step goals along the way, means you will be pushing yourself forward to ensure each goal is attained. Achieving your goal may take time, and you are going to face challenges along the way. There are going to be days when you don't want to take action. These are the days that your *why* should push you on and draw you forward into action.

Your *why* prompts you to persevere and overcome days of doubt. There are days when you doubt you will ever attain your goal due to your age, social status, culture, career, or some undefined fear. To stay on track and stay motivated, it may be time to redefine your goal so that it has personal meaning and significance for you.

Consider what attaining this goal will mean to you personally. Is this goal in line with your values and beliefs? Will achieving the next smaller goal bring you closer to your long-term goal? Will it be necessary to adjust the next step due to unforeseen circumstances or new knowledge?

Take time out to be brutally honest with yourself. Are you just looking for an excuse? Explore your core needs and rediscover the *why* for each goal along your path to attaining your dream goal, which served as your motivation at the start of your journey. If you revisit the true *why*, you will get back on track to reach for the gold, even if it means you need to adjust a few steps along the way.

2. You Have an Unrealistic Action Plan

You have broken your goal into small, manageable, and achievable goals. Look at this as milestone goal setting. Focusing on achieving each of these milestones and then celebrating each achievement is the best way to stay motivated.

Don't feel intimidated by the seemingly vast effort required to meet your goal. As the wise saying goes, you can only eat an elephant one bite at a time! Take your small action steps toward your milestones on time, every time, and once in a while, you may allow yourself the pleasure of looking back at how far you have already progressed.

3. You are Not Being Held Accountable

Growth and change are often uncomfortable and challenging. Most of us would rather stay in our comfort zones. Allow yourself to evolve beyond your comfort zone in order to achieve your goals. You don't have to rely on willpower alone; bring in reinforcements.

Invest in a personal trainer or coach. Often, simply the knowledge of being accountable for your performance gives you enough motivation to stay on course. At times when you are feeling less motivated, your coach will be there to provide much-needed inspiration and remind you of your ultimate goal.

If you cannot afford a coach, involve people you care about in your goal planning. When people care about you, they want you to succeed, so make them part of your personal cheerleading team.

4. Obstacles Make You Give Up

Obstacles are an inevitable part of life, and it is often the surest way that strength of character and the resolve to persevere is built. This strength of character and resolve to persevere will be strengthened every day as you deal with new obstacles along your journey.

Planning ahead for challenges prepares you to face them head-on and not be blindsided. Staying on track and knowing what potential barriers may arise will ensure your success.

When setting your SMART goals (description below), list the potential challenges that may arise and brainstorm different ways to overcome each challenge. If you consider your options ahead of time, you will be prepared and know which course of action will have the best outcome.

Planning for challenges will go a long way to avoiding stress and mental overload and will keep you moving forward and upward toward attaining your goal.

5. Having an 'All or Nothing' Mentality

In the pursuit of our goals, there will be times when we slip or go off track. This is part of human nature. One slip is not going to derail a solid action plan. In fact, it should act as a motivator and an opportunity for growth. Ask yourself questions to determine the cause and effect, such as *why did I lose focus*, and *how can I prevent this from happening again?*

SMART goal-setting principles prompt you to review, realign, and restart. If you are constantly plagued by challenges, it is time to review. These questions will put you back on track.

Are my goals realistic? Should they be smaller and more attainable? And how can I learn from this and move forward?

SMART Goals

What is a SMART goal? SMART Goals have changed and gone through many transformations. Conceived by management consultant George T. Doran, a SMART goal is a goal that is consistent with the following parameters. As long as your goals do, you will achieve them.

S - Specific
M- Measurable
A - Attainable
R - Relevant
T - Timely

Specific: Having a specific goal makes you instantly aware of where you are going and what you want to achieve. Honing your skills on your target makes you focus on your target. If your goal is to run a marathon and you know the distance of a marathon is 26.2 miles, then you know you have a specific distance you need to train for.

Measurable: Making your goals measurable is the only sure way to track your progress. It automatically enhances your commitment to achieving your goals. By breaking up your ultimate goal into smaller measurable sections, you will quickly notice any deviations that can be corrected with small adjustments. As a runner, you can track your achievement in two ways, time or distance, or you can combine your tracking as time *and* distance. A marathon may be 26.2 miles, but you can track your progress after every quarter mile. This will keep your focus and motivate you to reach the next goal until you know you can go the distance.

Attainable: Setting goals that are achievable even though it requires effort will make the goal more tangible. Knowing the goal is within reach if you only train enough and push yourself a little farther each time increases the possibility of realizing your goal. As you achieve each goal, you can increase the difficulty level of your goals and not be afraid of failure.

Relevant: If you have defined your skillset and know what you can achieve, you will know how to set relevant and realistic goals. For example, if you want to run a marathon, it would be unrealistic to think that you can train well with a focus on swimming. Look at what you enjoy doing, then match it to your natural skillset and select a realistic goal.

Timely: Part of setting a goal includes establishing a time frame. This will show you whether your goal is achievable. Allow yourself a reasonable time frame in which to achieve your goal. If you are not attaining your goal despite your best efforts, it is time to go back to the start and reassess the goal. Reassess. Realign. Restart. This is where the smaller goals are especially valuable. Tracking your progress via these milestone goals will quickly alert you to anything that's off and will most often lead to making small adjustments rather than having to make a completely fresh start.

Apply These Tips to Revisit Your SMART Goals

Brainstorm Again What You Want to Achieve

Do a brainstorming session with yourself. Set a time limit for this session. Take five minutes to write down a list of goals you would like to achieve within the next 10 years. Use the 'rocking chair' test to evaluate your goals. Imagine yourself in a rocking chair at the age of retirement. What accomplishments make you proud? What is it you regret not doing? Answering these questions will give you an all-important glimpse into your innermost desires.

Prioritize Your Goals

When you are setting goals, be sure they are relevant. Setting irrelevant goals will waste your time and lead to failure. If you have a goal that is important to you, it will inspire you to achieve it. Having a tangible, relevant, achievable goal will make you work harder each day.

Visualize Your Success

Visualization is a powerful tool that allows your reality and your dreams to become one. The world in which we live is made up of energy particles, and where you concentrate your energy is the direction in which all energy flows. When you practice visualization daily, you will notice how your physical, mental, and spiritual energies become focused on your vision. Make a vision board with your success story, and see it become your reality.

Connect Your Goals to Purpose

Select your top goals for each year. Make sure these goals are achievable within 12 months. These goals must awaken a desire within you and be connected to a purpose in your life. The purpose of the goal is your *why*. In knowing your *why*, you will be able to develop the *how*.

Celebrate Your Success

Achieving your goals is an amazing feeling. Don't let a win go unnoticed. Celebrate!

When you reach a goal, even a small one, give yourself credit for the hard work you put in to reach that goal. Allow your brain to give you that much-needed dopamine boost and feel reenergized and ready to move on. Once you have celebrated, get right back on track and move toward your next goal.

Stay on Track

Affirmation is positive self-talk, and it is the scientifically proven way to create new neural connections. Science has found that it takes our brains 25 to 30 days to adapt to a new pattern of behavior. Positive affirmations and a positive mental image of your goal will form neural pathways in your subconscious mind. The anticipation of achieving a goal will boost endorphin creation in your brain, leaving you in a positive state of mind.

As a runner, you know that staying on track is how you win. Motivate yourself by using positive affirmations to stay happy, healthy, and focused. Here are some examples to prompt you to have some fun writing a list of affirmations:

- I have the courage to start, the courage to train, and the courage to succeed.
- I am motivated. I am persistent. I am successful.
- I believe that I can achieve what my mind can conceive.
- I see my dreams become a reality.
- I am confident and fearless.
- I believe in myself.
- I am confident in my abilities and skills.
- There is no limit to my success.
- I deserve the best.
- Every small step is a step toward my goal.
- I am capable of achieving more than I realize.
- I allow myself to take daring leaps toward my goals.
- I am committed to my goals.

Be Inspired!

Imagine winning the Boston and New York City Marathons and an Olympic silver medal! That is a reality for Meb Keflezighi, and he has revealed his roadmap to success in goal setting.

According to Meb, his physical achievements began psychologically. Meb says he simply thought, "I want to do this".

'Marathon Meb,' as he is affectionately known, says that in his experience, people start running to alleviate stress, not create more of it, especially if the rest of their life is already goal-oriented. The interesting thing is that you probably already have goals set for your running. It's human nature to strive toward a goal, and with running, you already have a plan. You have a general route in mind and a basic time to complete it. You have decided how many times you are going to run each week. Sure, these aren't stated and set goals, but they have already been formulated in your head.

Meb says that he sets his goals using five specific elements that make success easier to achieve. He shared the following approach in several interviews over the years.

Personal Meaning

Meb says the reason he became so successful and achieved his goals is that he decided what would motivate him to achieve his goal.

"Nobody ever told me, '*You have to win the 2014 Boston Marathon*' or '*You have to make the 2012 Olympic team.*" These were his own goals, he wanted to win Boston. These goals felt right to him and were in line with what he wanted to achieve with his running. He goes on to say that when you have a personal goal, you do what is necessary to achieve it.

If your goals are set with purpose and personal meaning, you will know what you are ready to do to achieve them. Your goals need to push you toward your achievement. If your goals are personal and not based on the expectations of others, you will find when you encounter an obstacle that you are ready for the challenge.

When you are faced with a challenge and the goal is not personal, you might find yourself asking, “Wait, why am I doing this?”, but a personal goal will motivate you to excel.

Specific Goals are the Best Goals

“In 2001, my main goal was to break the American 10,000 meters [record]. I needed to beat the record time of 27:20.56. That means my goal was specific up to the 100th of a second. Using those specifics, I knew what my pace had to be and how many workouts I had to hit. These specifics ensured that I excelled, and I won with a time of 27:13.98, a record that was unbroken until 2010.”

“If my goal had been more general, for example, I want to run well at Boston or I want to run faster in the 10 000 meters, any improvement would have fit in with this subjective goal. It is because my goal was so specific that I was motivated.”

Challenging but Realistic

“A victory in Boston was a realistic goal for me,” Meb says. “I had previously finished third and fifth, but this time I wanted to win. Achieving first place was challenging as I was the 15th-best runner in the field.”

"Trying to win certainly required reaching, given that the race was held two weeks before my 39th birthday and I had the 15th-fastest personal best in the field. An unrealistic goal for me would have been, 'I want to break the world record.' That would require cutting over five-and-a-half minutes from my personal best, and at this age, it is an unlikely goal."

Set your goals high enough that you are required to reach beyond your comfort zone. If you have already run a 2:05 half-marathon, making your next goal for a half-marathon of 2:05 won't be challenging as you have already achieved it. Similarly, setting an unrealistic time of 1:30 is unthinkable. Look at setting your goals in increments, for example, 1:59, 1:55, 1:50, and so on.

Long-distance running requires planning and realistic, incremental goal setting.

Timing: A Good Goal Includes a Time Frame

We are all motivated by deadlines, and having a set date and a structured plan to reach them makes them realistic and achievable.

Meb knows this. "In 2014, while I was training for the Boston Marathon, I told my wife that it was my last chance to win this marathon. However, had I said, 'I'd like to win the Boston Marathon someday,' I would never have been so motivated to win." You need to figure out where the 'sweet spot' lies. If you say, 'I want to run this year's New York City

Marathon,' and you only have two weeks to train, I will say good luck. Yet if you say, 'I want to run the 2025 New York City Marathon,' your goal's timeline is so distant, you won't be motivated to reach it."

Most runners need from three to six months to achieve their main goal, which is close enough to motivate them while still allowing enough time to train. Break your goal up into achievable sections. Decide on a month-end goal and then break it down further into weekly goals. If by the end of the month, you have not progressed, you have to reassess. Ask yourself, "What is holding me back? Is there something I should do differently? And am I sure this goal is realistic and achievable?".

Motivation: A Good Goal Keeps you Motivated

Meb writes down his goals so there is no ambiguity. His goals are set in black and white. 'I want to achieve this' is written where he can see it, and it motivates him.

Tell the people in your life about it. Having your friends and loved ones rooting for you ensures you will make the right choices and achieve your goal. If you have a training partner and want to cancel, your friend will say, "Wait, you're canceling our run? I thought you were training for a marathon."

"Leading up to the Boston Marathon in 2014, my wife, Yordanos, would check on me, saying, 'Shouldn't you be sleeping?'".

Family and friends are a support structure and will motivate you through the coming rough patches. They want what's good for you because they care. Who can have a better backup system than that?

Chapter 2
Developing a Holistic Approach in Your Thoughts and Actions

"Practice thinking like a Champion." — Marisa Peer

A holistic approach is a unique approach that fine-tunes your mind, body, and soul, taking into consideration all aspects of your physical, mental, and spiritual well-being, especially as it relates to your sport of choice—running.

Thoughts Matter

As a young girl, Marisa Peer was told that she was only capable of becoming a nanny, but Marisa had her own aspirations. She refused to fail and committed herself to learn to embrace empowerment and positive thinking. She believed in the woman she could become.

Marisa had a vision of whom she would become and achieved her goal through positive thinking and what she calls ‘the rule of the mind’. Marisa went on to become one of the UK’s most renowned therapists and a coach of Olympians.

Here are Some of Marisa’s Life-Changing Positive Thoughts:

- “Nobody is born with a success mindset. We learn and educate ourselves in order to think like a champion so that one day those thoughts become our reality.”
- “Belief without talent can take you further than talent without belief. But when you have both, you’re unstoppable.”
- “We work and hassle and fight for our dreams, and when we are there, standing at the door, we refuse to go in.”
- “Our fears take over our thoughts unless we learn to be bulletproof against them. Once we accept our doubts and we go forward anyway, we can celebrate our well-deserved success and the courage that got us there.”
- “Can you inspire others when you don’t really believe in yourself? Can you make this world a better place if you struggle to find your own voice?”
- “The hardest part is not changing our lives but changing our minds that ultimately create them. Be the person who talks, walks, thinks, reacts,

and acts as a champion, and soon enough you will realize you have just become one."

According to Marissa, "Words are powerful, and your mind is listening."

What is a Holistic Approach?

The holistic approach involves including components of body, mind, and soul, giving you a 360-degree perspective. This allows each runner to improve through these different aspects. The holistic approach incorporates all aspects of recovery, physically through rest or stretching as well as emotionally and mentally. The holistic approach requires that you look into how you prepare yourself mentally and emotionally for a run. What other psychological factors affect your runs? Fear, procrastination, motivation?

This approach requires that you see all aspects of the body, mind, and spirit working together as one. This enables synchronicity within each separate aspect of the body, mind, and spirit that brings about balance and well-being leading to harmony.

The Importance of a Holistic Approach to Sports Performance

There is an undeniably strong connection between the body, mind, and spirit. When you set a goal, you must address all of these areas to ensure complete success.

When looking at health and wellness, there is a clear correlation. When we are emotionally stressed or unwell, it impacts our physical health. Essentially, your emotional state, which includes your attitudes, beliefs, feelings, and thoughts, impacts your physical health.

Running holistically focuses on the optimal performance of the physiological, biomechanical, and psychological factors of the run. The interconnectedness and interaction of the individual parts optimize the performance and surpass the sum of the individual parts, creating an enhanced sense of well-being, increased health, and spiritual enjoyment that goes far beyond expectations.

Holistic running includes all aspects that result in a successful race, such as physical health, mental well-being, training, nutrition, tactics, motivation, rest, and recovery, as well as the right equipment.

To achieve a holistic run, personal trainers, coaches, physical therapists, nutritionists, sports psychologists, podiatrists, osteopaths, chiropractors, and sports equipment specialists all work together with one goal: the holistic success of the runner.

Scientific Benefits of a Holistic Approach

The scientific benefits of using a holistic approach, especially during endurance running such as a marathon, can be seen when observing runners.

During the past few decades, the focus has shifted from winning as the final goal to the range of benefits the holistic approach has on an athlete. Research has shown that a holistic approach is the best way to optimize sports performance as a whole.

This can be seen in the following ways:

- Increased athletic performance
- Improved balance
- Faster reaction time
- Injury reduction
- Improved tactical decision-making

Studies indicate that following holistic principles improves psychological aspects of well-being, reduces disease, and optimizes the quality of life.

Mind and body exercises like meditation, relaxation, hypnosis, visualization, and cognitive behavioral therapy can manage physical pain and reduce illness.

In athletes, these mind-body therapies can result in attaining their goals in their chosen sport while increasing their mental strength and resilience.

Why is a Holistic Approach Best?

As we grow and learn about life, health, and the mental and spiritual aspects of well-being, we come to realize that successful athletic performance requires focusing on all things because they are interrelated.

When a holistic-centered approach is coupled with a personalized approach to sports training and performance, the result is an athlete who is healthy, has great tactics, delivers strong performances, has good resilience, and exhibits an excellent mood and attitude. Also, rest and recovery of the athlete, physically and mentally, occur at a faster pace.

Practicing holistic training is the key to elite sporting success and gives the athlete a significant competitive advantage.

Activities to Boost Mind-Body Wellness

Practicing activities that support the interconnectedness of the mind, body, and soul will bring your inner self and your physical body into alignment. Practice these activities regularly, and begin to feel the difference in your daily life:

- Ensure your body is fueled with healthy food containing all the nutrients, vitamins, and minerals that it needs.
- Work on a deeper connection with others and yourself.
- Boost your self-love, happiness, and self-esteem by boosting it in others.
- Meditate, pray, pause, or do relaxing breathing exercises.

- Get enough nightly sleep.
- Make stress management a part of your daily routine.
- Be thankful, and practice gratitude and harmony in all aspects of your life.
- Walk or run outdoors, and train your mind to be aware of every moment.
- Train your mind to find a positive thought for every negative thought that crops up.
- Smile, and greet everyone you meet.
- Enjoy the beauty of noticing the small things.
- If your walking has to be indoors, visualize yourself painting on the blank wall.
- Listen to music while you exercise, changing your steps to match the rhythm.

Be Inspired!

Rio, August 14, 2016. The world is watching Usain Bolt in the lineup. He is moving in his characteristic Jamaican rhythm. The crowd cheers. Bolt looks energized, excited, and...happy.

Bolt is last out of the blocks, and his nemesis Justin Gatlin of the USA is in a clear lead. Approaching the halfway mark, Gatlin draws farther ahead. The crowd is waiting with bated breath. There are about 40 meters left. Bolt lets loose!

He effortlessly takes the gold and continues on his victory lap. He poses with mascots, takes selfies with fans, and gives his trainers to a young fan.

Bolt's energy is irresistible. His fans wait in anticipation to see what he is going to do next. How else is he going to spread his positive energy?

Positivity beats Anxiety!

Not so very long ago in the previous century, corporate management was convinced that anxiety made staff perform better and quicker. This was based almost solely on the old 'fight, flight, or freeze' response in the face of danger—in this case, the fear of not making a business target and losing a job. It all made perfect sense. The hormones that were released increased energy and thus performance.

The concept of Positive Psychology has, however, emerged in the decades since. The hormones dopamine and serotonin, released by the brain in anticipation of a happy experience, increase blood flow throughout the body. This automatically increases performance. So, the old question of what is better for increased performance, the carrot or the stick, has resurfaced. Does success make you happy, or does finding joy in what you are doing make you successful?

The German Sport University in Cologne took their research to athletes on the track and proved the power of positive psychology, according to Rory Darkin in his 'Running Free' blog in 2017. This research showed that happy runners performed significantly better in sprints than those induced into a state of anxiety or those with neutral mindsets at the start of their races.

Just imagine what a happy and excited demeanor can bring to the starting blocks of your holistically-trained mind, body, and spirit in any endeavor, whether you are going for gold or not!

Thanks to Usain Bolt, we have learned that a positive attitude fosters a positive mindset, and with a positive mindset, you can achieve your wildest dreams.

Bolt says his positive mindset is what makes him go the extra mile (or extra meters in his case) and shaves off those extra seconds.

So, How Does he Do It?

Bolt believes intrinsically in positive thinking. His formula is that happiness brings success, which is the opposite of what most people believe. In the business world and in life, the general belief is that success brings happiness. If that is how you think, stop, turn it around, and start believing that happiness is the key to success.

Research in the field of positive psychology has shown that positive emotions lead to enhanced performance and success in mind and body.

If you rewind the video and watch Bolt win again, you will note that it is almost as if he came alive as he won the race. He wasn't only smiling; his joy came from deep inside, just as it did at the start of the race. He wasn't anxious or stressed; he looked ready and excited. His happiness and positive attitude shone through like the sun.

How Does Positivity Make You Run Faster?

Emotions fuel performance, as shown by social psychology expert Dr. Barbara Fredrickson's Broaden and Build Theory of Positive Emotions.

Now take this one step further. Think of a situation when you were so stressed or anxious that you could almost not see a positive outcome. Conversely, think of a situation when you were confident and optimistic. You could see countless positive opportunities. Researchers have found that when you are optimistic, hormones such as dopamine and serotonin flood the brain. These chemicals, also called the 'happy hormones,' increase awareness in your brain and boost your self-confidence. Furthermore, your blood vessels dilate and blood rushes through your veins, into your muscles, and increases your physical performance.

Scientists at the German Sports University have been studying how mental performance is affected by anxiety and pleasure. The results show unequivocally that athletes who had a happy demeanor ran faster than athletes who were exposed to negativity.

Looking back at Bolt and his characteristic Jamaican joy, smiling at the crowd, we can conclude that if he was stressed or anxious, the race might have had a totally different outcome. His positivity, joy in running, and excitement of being at the Olympic Games sent a flood of endorphins through his body, shifting his performance into top gear and enabling him to win in eight one-hundredths of a second. Not only did he win, but the rush of 'happy hormones' made him a crowd-pleaser as he relished being part of crowd selfies with his fans during his victory lap. What a moment, what joy, what a spectacular finale!

Chapter 3

Winning the Mental Game

"If you say yes in your heart and mind, and say it in your mouth, then you can perform."
— Eliud Kipchoge

Mental power is the key to a fulfilled life, especially in sports. You may be a brilliant athlete, but when you harness the power of the *mind,* you excel. We now know that the mind, body, and spirit are one, and when they work together, there is absolutely no stopping you from attaining great results. The importance of a winning mindset will take you over the finish line in one easy stride.

Mindset: An Overview

Have you ever taken a moment to think about the power of the mind? Consider for a moment the stories you have heard about an athlete who was paralyzed and told they would never walk again, never mind run. And yet they did.

The Power of the Mind

The power of the mind is unequaled. It has an amazing effect on the physical body. Considering the size of the brain in relation to the rest of the body, it is amazing what control this organ has over the rest of the body. It functions as the boss that triggers orders and adjustments to tissues, veins, muscles, and in fact, every cell in your body. It physically controls the working of your bodily functions, from breathing to hormones, glands, muscles, organs, and everything in between.

The brain itself is in turn influenced and controlled by our consciousness, according to many scientists and neurologists, although others believe that consciousness is firmly seated in the brain.

Regardless of where consciousness is found in the body, one's mindset accounts for a major distinction between achieving success or falling short.

If you are serious about achieving success, learn to master your mind.

From Full Paralysis to a Marathon in 10 Months

In 2013, Diane Owens's son Alex was diagnosed with neurofibromatosis (NF), a disease that causes tumors to grow on every nerve in the body, including the brain. The disease varies in symptoms and seriousness, and it can be fatal.

Diane decided to become a marathon runner to raise money to combat this disease. She said at the time, "I promised my son Alex I would run marathons for him." Diane ran a 10-mile race by October of that year. The bug had bitten her, and she ran marathon after marathon raising money for NF. By the end of 2015, after completing a 7-mile, 10-mile, four half-marathons, and three full marathons, Diane felt she could call herself a runner.

Diane was Alex's champion, and her motivation—a personalized goal of running for Alex—kept pushing her, putting one foot in front of the other when she felt like giving up.

On January 23, 2016, Diane started feeling as if sharp pins were piercing her skin. She went to the doctor for a checkup just before her fourth marathon. Within a week, she was paralyzed, and the doctors confirmed Guillain-Barré syndrome (GBS), a disorder that causes the immune system to attack the nerve cells. Diane's case was bad. Although her mind was sharp, all of her limbs, including her mouth and eyelids, couldn't move, and she could hardly breathe.

Diane thought of Alex. Who would be his champion now? Who would raise money for his treatment?

When Diane was taken to rehab, she couldn't move at all

but decided that she was a warrior who could overcome this. Little by little, feeling returned to her body. Her limbs were coming alive again.

She started pedaling on a small foot-pedal exerciser and in her head, told herself, *I am going to run again.*

While still in the hospital, Diane signed up for three marathons. The doctors thought she was crazy. They warned her that she was going to require therapy for at least a year and, even then, there was no guarantee she could run again. But Diane's promise to her son, her resolve, and her strong mind proved them all wrong.

Diane was discharged in October, and her first outdoor run was on April 9, 2016.

In 2016, Diane completed four races with the grand finale at the California International Marathon in December.

What is Mindset?

Mindset is a set of beliefs that you have developed over time. It includes your belief and value systems, and it is how you make sense of the world in which you live. Your mindset influences your thoughts, behavior, and how you view the people around you. It even influences the physical functioning of your body.

How is it Formed?

Your mindset is formed as you experience situations, emotions, and behavior, including the way you are treated and the behavior you are taught at home, at school, and in social environments. A mindset is an established attitude toward a certain action, object, or group, influenced by one's cultural values, philosophy, and worldview. Having a specific mindset can be due to a worldview that is followed by peers or parents, or it can be your own philosophy of life as determined by what you have seen, heard, and experienced.

Why It's Important to Have the Right Mindset

In any area of life, it is important to cultivate a positive mindset as this is what will make you succeed in whatever you undertake. As an athlete who takes part in competitive sports, a positive mental attitude is what gives you the edge. Yes, training for your sport is imperative, but your attitude is what sets you apart.

As a marathon athlete, you know only too well how much stamina it takes to push your body that last stretch and across the finish line. The difference between getting the gold or not is found in your attitude. Sometimes when it feels that your legs just cannot go another stretch, it is the mental push that gives you the final burst of energy to override your doubts.

Your emotions on race day can affect your performance. If you are sad or anxious, your frame of mind will not be that of a winner. However, if you are happy and excited and picture a good run, chances are that you will do well in the marathon.

If you are a serious marathon runner, you need to give as much credence to your attitude as your stamina.

Many serious marathon runners and other athletes have an entire team supporting them, including a mental coach. Coaches like these teach you mental strategies that reverse negative thinking and get rid of limiting beliefs while showing you ways to increase and uplift your energy and physical performance.

The Importance of Beliefs

Success and the personal drive to achieve a set goal are directly related to our belief systems. Creating and maintaining a positive belief system is integral to living a happy and harmonious life. Events and experiences that we have had in the past created the mindset that is prevalent in the decisions we make. Depending on the current belief system we have, we make decisions. These decisions can either put us on the path to success or hamper our plans for the future.

"Whether you believe you can do a thing or not, you are right."
— Henry Ford (1947 in *Reader's Digest*)

This idea has been tossed about in various versions ever since the Roman author Virgil wrote in his famous book, the *Aeniad: "For they can conquer who believe they can."* Henry Ford's words coined the adage perfectly to express how your mindset aligns the outcome of your efforts with your thoughts and beliefs.

Our brains are programmed to find opportunities

Our minds have been preprogrammed to find opportunities for success and are constantly filtering information that supports our beliefs. If we have a negative outlook on life, our minds will find information that confirms that negativity. This will lead to an unenjoyable life that reinforces our belief that our world is filled with negative aspects.

In the same way, our minds can instead search for positive affirmations and use this to program body, mind, and soul toward positive outcomes. This is one of the main reasons that life coaches and motivational speakers encourage the use of daily positive affirmations. As noted earlier, positive affirmations create a feedback hyperloop that programs our minds to find opportunities in which we will shine, *running* toward success in our personal as well as professional lives.

Belief in Others

We live in a world populated by people from all walks of life, with different belief systems, different values, and different cultures. As we communicate with people, we tend to gravitate toward those who have the same beliefs and value systems that we have. At times, we learn immeasurably valuable lessons from others, and at other times, we see people exhibiting the kind of behavior that shows us a type of character that we don't want to emulate.

Building relationships with people throughout our lives enriches our experience of life. You may find a person you particularly admire, and this person could have a positive influence on your life. This is the kind of person who would be good as a mentor. For example, if you want to be successful in business, find someone who has attained business success and follow the example of their goals and actions.

Self-Confidence is Elevated

The old question of which comes first, the chicken or the egg, can be used as an example when we look into the building of self-confidence. Does self-confidence come first, or does belief come first? What is certain is that both self-confidence and belief are interrelated and affect each other. If you believe that accomplishing a specific goal is not possible, then you will most probably fail. If you have the self-confidence that grew out of a belief that you can achieve that goal, you will achieve it. This self-confidence strengthens our neural pathways, and the next time we are faced with a similar situation, we will believe even more firmly that we can overcome any challenge.

In his book, *The Power of Self-Confidence,* Brian Tracey explains how to develop 100% self-confidence by conditioning our minds to believe that there is a positive side to any situation we face. He writes that positive affirmations enable the mind to change from a negative belief system to a positive belief system.

Gain Peace of Mind and Reduce Stress

By building self-confidence and believing in our abilities, we are ready to face any challenge and have an innate sense that we will succeed. In fostering a positive attitude and mindset, we know that we have the ability to achieve new goals and succeed in everything life throws at us. Having self-confidence in our abilities reduces the daily stress and anxiety that we are faced with at work and at home.

As our self-confidence is boosted by positive affirmations, situations that might have previously resulted in anxiety will simply become another challenge that we know we need to face. Potential issues like public speaking, conflict with colleagues, and deadlines will no longer result in nervous pressure and anxiety attacks. Instead, they will become an exciting challenge to overcome and a time to grow in our personal and professional lives.

This is good news for our overall health as well. Did you know that stress results in the release of hormones such as cortisol, adrenalin, and prolactin, among others? Dealing with constant stress puts your life at risk and affects your ability to perform a required task.

When you have peace of mind because you have the self-confidence and positivity to deal with situations, your mental and physical stress levels are reduced, which automatically results in better health.

Take the first steps in turning your mind into a positive state by challenging yourself daily. Remind yourself that there are no limitations on what you can achieve except the limitations you set for yourself. The first step is to contemplate any negative ideas or thoughts you might have about a person, event, experience—or, dare I say it, about yourself! Use this thought to ask yourself whether this is a fact or simply your perception. Now reframe this event into a positive by looking at it from a different perspective. Once you have reframed the event, analyze what you have learned. In the future, when you are faced with similar negative thoughts, break down the situation and reframe it. This takes practice, but once you have mastered the art of reframing, you will face the world and yourself with a completely positive mindset.

What follows are some pointers from world-renowned sports coaches that you can use to ensure you achieve your goal.

Developing Healthy Self-Esteem

Self-esteem is an essential component of success that comes from self-perception and self-love. To feel worthy of gaining success, you must feel worthy of achieving your goals.

This means you must feel capable of achieving the goals you set for yourself. A strong and positive mindset is the key to developing healthy self-esteem. Self-esteem includes the spectrum of feelings and convictions that we harbor about ourselves as well as our internal beliefs and value sets in our dealings with others. Good self-esteem gives you the courage to go after the goals you set for yourself in life and achieve them. It also gives you the courage not to focus on your losses but on how far you have come when a goal remains out of reach—and the courage to review and adjust your perspective and lead a healthy and fulfilled life.

Formulating a Winning Perspective

We all know the adage of whether one sees the glass half-empty or half-full. This perfectly illustrates whether we view things in a positive or negative light. When we deliberately apply this test to an event or circumstance, it soon becomes clear whether we see a positive or negative outcome even if it was dormant in our subconscious. The type of mindset you have is reflected in your perspective, your attitude, and your behavior toward everything in life. Your inherent beliefs and values thus manifest in the way you view and approach an event and the world around you. An optimistic mindset will inevitably aim you in a positive direction. A negative mindset will manifest in a defeatist attitude and conduct even before you begin.

Harnessing Drive

Our bodies are wonderfully made and unbelievably strong, not only physically but mentally and spiritually. The cells in our bodies were made to regenerate after an injury. Look at your physical body and how quickly it regenerates after a fall. You may be running on an unfamiliar trail and lose your footing. Maybe you just scratch up your legs, but in more extreme cases, you may break an ankle. Even then, with the right care, the break will heal and the cells in your ankle are regenerated within a matter of weeks.

Harnessing the power of your mind to achieve your goals gives you the ultimate determination to push through any obstacles that are barring your path to success. Your drive and your energy will be in alignment with your vision to reach the goal you have set for yourself.

This power can be seen especially in the case of injury. Some people recover from an injury faster than others. Researchers have studied athletes in many sports for decades and have concrete proof that an athlete who lives a healthy lifestyle with a powerful vision of attaining their goals can rarely be stopped. There is even quantitative and qualitative proof that harnessing the power of visualization increases the natural healing in all of your cells, including your muscles.

People with the ability to focus all of their efforts on their primary goals find within themselves the strength and commitment to their higher purpose. They surpass the natural boundaries of comfortable zones through the sheer force of their internal drive.

Face Adversity—Head-On

As you strive toward success in any field, you are bound to encounter challenges and adversity. This adversity will appear when you least expect it, and this is where a keen and focused mind will challenge the adversity head-on with confidence.

Your mindset, strengthened by mental and spiritual growth, has developed along with your physical body, and now, the three form a unit that is an indestructible force. Any challenge can be overcome by the mind, spirit, and body as their union creates a truly resilient mindset.

This resilience, when challenged, reminds me of the words of the legendary world leader, Nelson Mandela: “Do not judge me by my successes; judge me by how many times I got back up.”

The amazing thing about having a truly resilient mindset is that you will inadvertently apply this mindset across all areas of your life—your sports, your career, your family life, your social life, and your spiritual growth.

Achieving the Underlying Goal

Goals often involve multifaceted processes. They are complex, with the final and most important goal being the ultimate goal or indicator of fulfillment in life. Mental staying power is what determines whether the goal will be achieved or fall by the wayside after a difficult challenge. It includes mental and physical determination and relies on the person's internal motivation or self-talk to keep them on track. Once a challenging goal has been reached, new goals and successes become the focal point.

What is Positive Thinking?

Positive thinking results when you combine all of your personal beliefs, emotions, values, and attitude and focus them on positivity. Positive thoughts expect the good to happen, while negative thoughts are cringing at the possibility that something bad *might* happen.

Positive thinkers develop a mindset that is in tune with the good and the positive in the universe and people who firmly believe in this. People who have mastered this are able to leverage the law of attraction. The law of attraction in a positive mindset creates a hyperloop that brings even more positive thoughts and actions into your life.

What Positive Thinking is Not

Positive thinking is most often not a miracle that magically takes over our psyches, especially as trauma is part of daily life in today's world. Although there are people who seem to have been born with a built-in positive attitude, the truth is usually much more complicated than that and even encompasses the controversial age-old question of *nature versus nurture*.

Many adults with positive attitudes have acquired them through practice and perseverance as they set achievable life goals and get back up to reset them when there are setbacks. And then the day comes when it has become their nature to see the growth and opportunities hidden in problems and adversity. That is the day when positive thinking starts pushing them away from the fear of failure and toward setting goals that seem just a tiny bit out of reach. That's the day they go for gold!

Positive thinking focused on a sound action plan and an achievable goal is not something that is going to fall from the sky though. Positive people with goals and plans to achieve those goals will enjoy the journey and every goal when they reach it because they know they have planned and worked hard.

Benefits of Positive Thinking

1. Empower Yourself

This might sound easy to some, but for others, it may be a real struggle.

The belief in your ability to achieve a good job, a good marriage, and other successes in life is a part of your inner being. It was formed, nurtured, battered, bent, and praised through experiences over the course of your life thus far.

The way you act when faced with a challenge shows your inner being. Do you blame others when things go wrong? Do you look for a solution? Do you take stock of the issue and take control of your reactions? Successful people take control. They work from an inner belief that there is a solution to everything, and the solution must simply be found.

Remember that in life, the only thing you can control is yourself, and it is how you act in adverse situations and circumstances that define you. Once you understand that you have control over your actions and reactions in life and that you can change the outcome, you are harnessing the full power of positive thinking.

2. Take Control of Your Mental State

Notice your body language when you are having a bad day. You don't stand up tall and straight. You might slouch in a chair. Your body has all the telltale signs. Chances are you will avoid contact with others, and if you do speak, it will be in monosyllables. This creates a poor feedback loop and all the negativity from your body language ends up as part of your mindset. This has created a negative mindset that will carry on until you do a total mind, body, and spirit reset.

Applying positive thinking holistically involves taking all aspects of your body, mind, and spirit into consideration. Think about how you present yourself to the world. Take pride in the way you walk, talk, and dress. Superficially, we can all but disregard the adage 'don't judge a book by its cover.' The fact is that there is seldom enough time in the proverbial rat race to delve deeper into the pages for hidden gems. So, the cover presented to us up front is what most people in the world today rely on for making a first judgment.

Nonverbal cues such as standing with your hands in your pockets and fidgeting with your hair, clothes, or fingers are a no-go zone. These things are considered rude in most cultures. They are seen by people you meet to be proof of low self-esteem and disrespect. People who are serious about their lives don't want to do business or engage in new friendships with people who don't present the right image.

Once you have unlearned these nonsensical habits, you will develop a naturally confident attitude to go with your new self-assured attitude. Once you are used to standing calmly and exuding your natural intrinsic power, a positive mindset will naturally follow.

Your natural positivity will create a hyperloop, and you will exhibit this new confident self-image to everyone around you. The more you exude confidence and positivity, the more you will attract positive interactions with the world and the people with whom you come into contact. When you have realized this role in your life, the role you were always meant to have, you will find the time and gain perspective about how to give back to the world and others. Part of the wonderful reward will appear in the form of changing others' lives by your example—a great reason for a gratitude run!

3. Adjust Your Mindset

Maintaining a healthy body is only one part of the solution to peace and internal harmony. It all starts with your mindset, which influences your entire being. Your mind is the place of origin of every action and reaction that flows throughout your body. If you are prone to a negative mindset, your reality will move in a way that confirms your negative thought patterns. Every action, no matter how small, will seem like a mountain that is impossible to climb.

Take, as an example, an everyday experience. You arrive at the supermarket, you can't find parking, and when at last you do, it is far from the entrance to the store—or, as a friend of mine calls it, the bleeding-nose section of the parking lot. In the shop, you start looking for the items on your list. The great marketing gods have moved the stock around again, and you have to search for the spice refills, which are now at the back of the spice shelf. You find that several of the items on your list are out of stock. You go to the checkout, where you are greeted by a surly staff member who takes her time ringing up your items, hoping that the next customer will depart to another checkout when she sees how slow things are moving.

At last, you leave the supermarket and load your groceries into the car. The drive home is surprisingly traffic-free, and you arrive home safely.

Are you going to spend the rest of your evening ruminating about all the negatives you experienced throughout the supermarket trip, or are you going to make a cup of tea and take a moment to be thankful for all the positive things that happened that day?

Choosing whether to reflect on and suffocate in the negatives in your life rather than the positives is something you can control. As noted earlier, the only thing in life we can control is ourselves and our reactions to actions or events.

This is a time to choose to live in the moment. What has passed is over and done with, and you cannot change it. Consciously focus on the positive events and experiences in your life and refrain from rehashing any negative thoughts. Begin to cultivate an abundance mindset that is filled with gratitude and hopeful expectations to see how your universe moves to align with your new positivity.

4. Form New Positive Habits

To effect change in your life, you have to take stock of your current emotions, behavior, and actions. To harness the power of positive thinking, stop, reflect, and discard that which is not in tune with your new attitude. Let the traffic rush past, let the phone ring. It's time for you to put yourself first. Allow the miracle of positivity in the universe to flow into and through you and become the vehicle for all things positive. That is not to say you need to be a bright-red, smiling lollypop anime every day, but assess what you have learned and put it into practice.

Forming new habits is difficult and well-nigh impossible if you don't have a realistic, brutally honest perspective regarding your current position. It is time to ask yourself the difficult questions, the questions we avoid, such as these regarding your job:

- What sends you into a spiral of self-doubt?
- What are the things that cause you to spiral into negativity?

- Which thoughts take you to that dark corner of your mind?
- Does thinking about work make you irritable?
- Do you find yourself making calculations of what you have contributed to the company and the recognition you have received if any?
- Do your superiors appreciate your skillset and recognize your input?
- Weigh all of these thoughts and make a decision as perhaps it's time to move on.
- This is not to say be hasty and don't think about the consequences, but perhaps the time has come to implement positive changes.

As renowned life coach Tony Robbins put it: "If you're not growing, you're dying." If you are unhappy, unfulfilled, or feeling negative about any aspect of your life, the time has come to consider your options and make some life-changing decisions. Be firm in your resolve to stop letting your mind wander into negative thought patterns. You can be sure that the negativity in one area will eventually permeate through the positives in other aspects of your life, making your whole worldview dark and negative. Refocus your mind and energy toward positive, joyful, and empowering habits.

Train your mind to substitute negative thought patterns with positive, mind-enhancing thoughts. As we have seen, according to scientists, it takes your mind just 25 to 30 days to develop a new habit. Don't let anything stop you.

Start today.

5. Choose Your Words with Care

The subconscious is a realm of the mind that has been explored since ancient times and more recently by modern psychiatrists with knowledge accumulated through many centuries. Freud, known as the Father of Psychoanalysis, did extensive research on the topic. He even observed his daughter, Anna, to see how the brain develops when presented with experiences at different ages. Following Freud, Carl Jung ventured deeply into the subconscious mind.

It was proved that our subconscious mind accumulates knowledge from both verbal and nonverbal expressions of thoughts and actions. It is therefore essential to choose your vocabulary carefully to match your positive visions and ambitions. Words that you use in conversation with others and words that you use as self-talk have a deep impact on your mind. Decades of studies have proven that positive self-talk improves your mental, physical, and spiritual state. Positive self-talk is used in various therapies and, again, brings the hyperloop into play. What you see, hear, and speak hyperloops and comes back as what you hear and process, and without knowing it, you have created a positive (or negative) hyperloop.

6. Think Before you Speak

This one we have all heard before, either from our parents, our teachers, or other adults. But have you considered what it really means? If the use of positive words and thoughts can bring positivity into your life, find a person you admire and watch them closely.

It can be a celebrity, a marathon runner, a businessman, a teacher, or even someone in your peer group. Does this person have a set of worthy values that they live by? When they address a crowd, television crew, or reporters, do they stand up straight and answer politely even when the question is unfair or unseemly? Watch how the person treats others, even if there aren't reporters watching. Are they still kind and caring? Now, remember the feedback hyperloop. If you follow this person's career long enough, you will see that all the positivity put out into the world by them will at some stage come right back. That is the power of positive words and the positive hyperloop.

Power of Visualization and the Marathon

What is Visualization?

Visualization is referred to as 'imagery' in competitive sports. Imagery uses all five senses to bring your sport into the realm of realism. Elite athletes have shared their secrets of winning with journalists, saying that when you focus on the entire process, this multisensory technique cultivates a competitive edge.

What is Imagery?

Imagery using all five senses creates such a realistic picture in the mind that it almost feels as if you can step into the picture. This process can be practiced anywhere and anytime. For an athlete, learning to completely shift into an alternate mind space is extremely valuable. When the crowd is roaring and the pressure is on, imagery enables you to calm your mind and focus on the race and the result.

Researchers who study athletes and their performance have found that visual imagery, when combined with kinesthetics —in this case, the perceptions of one's body motions— greatly improves performance.

Elite athletes, especially those who compete at the Olympic level, enhance and improve both performance and rehabilitation through this method. Imagery is referred to by coaches and the athlete's training team as a mental rehearsal of race day.

Sports psychology researchers have studied the impact of imagery for decades. In 2017, a paper was published that stated unequivocally that athletes who use imagery as part of their training excel regardless of age, sex, or athletic ability. It was also observed that focusing on the process and not the goal makes achieving the goal easier.

Visualizing Success

Visualization intensifies the emotions and physical responses that an athlete draws on before a race. These techniques bring about a heightened state of mind and awareness of their bodies.

According to researchers, athletes who have practiced visualization and imagery and 'intend' the outcome of the race are usually those who realize their dreams. These athletes are like Usain Bolt—confident before the run and confident after the win. They visualize the outcome, and an innate calm seems to let them exclude any distractions so they can focus on the race.

While the athlete visually creates the scene, they experience all of the sights, sounds, and smells of previous best race performances and outcomes. The athlete embodies the emotions of a winner, and with every stride, pictures the details of breaking the ribbon and taking the medal.

Repeat Performances

Once an athlete has learned to use imagery and visualization, their mind will be trained to naturally recall the feelings, emotions, and smells they experience while attaining the goal. The more the athlete employs these techniques, the easier it becomes. The athlete finds that switching from external imagery to internal imagery is more motivational and more likely to produce an excellent performance.

Once again, scientists have come forward with proof. They proved that these athletes are able to improve physical and psychological reactions when faced with certain scenarios.

Repeated visual imagery has the ability to inspire confidence. It removes nervousness and makes performing during competitions an exhiJeanneting and joyful experience.

Use Your Senses

The smell of freshly-baked bread or cookies may take you right back to sitting at your grandmother's kitchen table as a child, salivating for that exquisite taste of still-warm cookies. In the same way, feeling the energy of the crowd, smelling the fresh morning air, and seeing the finish-line banner can trigger imagery of your best run. It places you in 'the zone,' and when you are in 'the zone,' you know the race is yours and only yours. This is the time to let loose. Everything you have trained for is within your grasp, and nothing of what you had to give up making all those training days happen can take away from the exhiJeannetion of this moment. Let loose and go for your personal best!

Using guided imagery, mental rehearsals, and visualization maximizes your efficiency during training runs and on race days. In today's world of champion athletes where the win is often measured in hundredths of a second, athletes cannot rely on their physical stamina and natural skills alone.

Guided imagery, visualization, and other techniques will maximize the effectiveness of your skills in our technologically-driven world. Even winning by a hundredth of a second remains a win and, more importantly, you know you have done it. The next time, you can visualize doing it faster!

Shape Your Mind and Body

The mind controls all parts of the body and spirit. It is therefore no wonder that it plays a big role in shaping your personal and professional life. People have mistakenly formed the habit of calling the mind positive or negative when really the correct terms are trained and untrained.

We are faced with challenging choices daily and need to have the confidence to make the right choices. The mindset that we have cultivated, such as a positive or negative mindset, will influence the choice we make. Our success or failure is dependent on the trained or untrained mind.

Training our minds to look at the positive elements in our daily lives will help us to make positive choices when we are faced with challenges.

Cultivating a positive mindset takes time, effort, and practice, but it allows you to shift your mindset from negative to positive.

According to Tony Robbins, "Whatever you hold in your mind on a consistent basis is exactly what you will experience in life."

Chapter 4

Unlocking Your Physical Strength

"Take care of your body. It's the only place you have to live." — Jim Rohn

After conquering the mind, the next step is to tackle physical strength. Remember, a healthy mind resides in a healthy body. This chapter will help you fill your 'runner's toolbox' and provide insight into training plans and equipment.

Why Run?

There are many reasons why people run, and all of them are unique and specific to the person who chooses running as a favored activity. They may like running competitively or running casually with a friend three times a week. Running is different for everyone, and there is no 'correct' way; there is only the ideal way that suits you and your lifestyle.

The white horses of the Camargue come to mind when I think about running, and the same feelings are invoked when I watch a joyful runner. The strength, style, and movement of such a runner reflect absolute freedom and elation oozing from their inner being, joining the mind, body, and soul in one graceful action.

You can see how the muscles harmonize in rhythm to a physically beautiful symphony. Then you look at the face of the runner and can almost feel the intensity in their being. They want to win this race and take home the gold, and nothing less will do. It is all too easy to forget the amount of training that goes into running.

This is the person who identifies as a serious runner. Their goal is to reach the top, whether in sprints or marathons. If your ambition is to get fit or perhaps lose some weight, this is a commitment, and for you it is serious. On the flip side, 'serious' to a marathon runner means they have a total commitment to proper training, nutrition, and lifestyle. These are the runners we love to watch on television or in online video clips. Their total commitment is unbelievable and inspiring.

The reasons for taking up running are as vast as the sport itself. Perhaps you and some other runners where you live have decided to form a running group to get fit and enjoy some company. Running is a great way to calm your mind after a stressful day at work or even to organize your thoughts for your new business idea if you are an entrepreneur. Running gives you time to focus with each stride. When you run and allow your mind to be inspired, you may come up with that million-dollar idea you have been searching for. The benefits of running are endless when you let your mind go and your body moves in rhythmic strides.

People run for a multitude of reasons, and here are some that might apply to you:

- As you run, your body releases endorphins, and you may experience a 'runner's high.'
- Running is known to be one of the best stress relievers.
- Losing weight is difficult, but when you hit the road and the weight falls off, you will be happy you started running.
- Running improves aerobic fitness.
- Running alone might seem lonely, but to some people, this is the time that they can completely immerse themselves in peace and solitude.
- Running can become your time of reflection and decision-making.
- Running promotes better overall health and has been shown to improve lung capacity, increase metabolic rates, lower cholesterol levels, and decrease the risk of osteoporosis.

Instant Bond with Running

I bonded with running immediately. My friend asked me to join her on a run, and I agreed. I had the wrong trainers, the wrong underwear, and many other things that I would now be able to advise new runners to take care of. At the end of the run, I somehow felt a deep change had taken place within me, and I was eager to further explore running.

The exhiJeannetion, the magic, and the excitement of my first run opened up a totally new world for me, and I knew that I wanted to become a runner. I now had a new goal. This sent me on an internet search for everyone and everything involved with running. There was so much information that I did not know where to begin. Then I decided to approach running as I would approach a business task. If you are a property developer and want to build a perfect skyscraper, you call in the best architectural firms and give them a brief. You call them back with an agreed time to discuss which design and budget suit you.

I searched for different options, from training plans to group classes and private coaches. Your budget and your goal will determinate your choice, but for running a marathon, I would recommend a coach or, at minimum, joining a running club to leverage the expertise of others.

Even if you hire a running coach, it is important to remain a curious student and educate yourself further, such as on matters of nutrition. The coach is there to give you pointers, but because we all have unique nutritional needs, learn as much as you can about yours. You are the only one who knows what your body needs as well as your likes and dislikes. I found that the more I learned about nutrition, the more I knew what to feed my body to fuel it optimally. And even today, that is my biggest hurdle.

I was off to the races, so excited to be a part of the frenzied pre-run jitters that happens backstage, before the run, the part that the adoring crowds never see. As you come out to take your place on the starting line, you become calm, collected, and focused, and nothing will get you off your game.

You are a runner. You think like a runner. You behave like a runner. And in that moment, you are not only a runner but the most important runner on the line.

Running the World

The world of runners has changed so much during the past century that wherever your area of interest lies, there is sure to be a type of running that resonates with you. Millions of people around the world enjoy running as a form of pure exercise or as a time to mull over the events of their day, one step at a time.

One of many things that make running one of the best physical activities is that you can pack your running shoes if you go on a business trip, and they will be there for you to slip on after your stressful presentation or meeting. There is no heavy equipment to lug around in your baggage, you don't have to find a partner (as you do for tennis and some other sports), and you don't have to find a gym near your hotel. You have your gym in your bag. What is even more exciting is that you get to run in different places. If you are visiting a coastal city, run on the beach. If you are staying in a wooded area, a trail run through the woods is one of nature's most soul-healing experiences.

Many yoga gurus recommend a walk or a meditative run through the woods. According to their beliefs, the healing quality of nature soothes your soul.

Find the Right Fit

There are so many types of running, a newbie can be dazed by all the words and terms runners use. The best way to navigate the waters is to research. In this case, the internet is your friend, but don't limit yourself to online searches. Follow them up with personal visits to tracks, clubs, and events. This will ensure you pick the right kind of running and the right people to run with for you.

Road Running

Road running is one of the most popular types of running. It's convenient, and the smooth surfaces keep you from tripping and falling face-first on the trail. Road running is the easiest way for runners to begin their running journey. Fitting road running into your schedule is easy—just tie up your trainers, don your running gear, and hit the road! There is nothing wrong with starting off like this, especially if you can find nice quiet roads to run on. However, for those who live in a bustling city, road running is not always the greatest idea. You will have pedestrians in your way and cars rushing by honking their horns, so this experience might put you off running totally. Therefore, take the time to consider some other options.

Treadmill Running

Treadmills provide an excellent alternative to road running as there are no cars, bikes, or pedestrians to get in the way. Another bonus is that whether it is pouring outside or the temperature is a ridiculous 100 degrees in the shade, you can still get your training session in.

Running on a treadmill also gives you a slight amount of bounce-back, which makes it easier on your joints. Treadmills are multiple settings that you can adjust—not only the speed but the angle (to simulate a steep or gradual incline).

My favorite advantage of treadmill running is that I can play my favorite workout jams. They energize me, and I don't have to be on the watch for distracted vehicle drivers, cyclists, or pedestrians. And last but not least, I have my nutrition handy and don't need to carry fluids or snacks with me.

Trail Running

For nature lovers, there is trail running. You can choose to combine your twin passions of nature and running. There is nothing as beautiful as hearing the birds singing all around you, the wind blowing wisps through your hair, and the rustling of the leaves and brambles. Trail runs are usually done on hiking trails, and the terrain varies, ranging from arid flats to mountainous rainforests. And trail runners enjoy the excitement of leaping over logs, crossing small streams, and climbing steep hills. Identify 'runnable' trails nearest your home or workplace so that you can make trail running a regular feature of your running routine rather than an occasional getaway to a distance park.

Track Running

Running tracks can be found at sports clubs, community centers, or most commonly, high school and college campuses. The benefit of track running is that you can train for shorter distances. Standard track races are from 100 meters to 10,000 meters (10K). You can choose an event like the 100-meter dash to hone your skills and then move up to longer distances as you feel ready. A 100-meter dash is a great way to establish whether you are a fast runner and should concentrate on sprints or whether you should look at long-distance track races or take up endurance running such as marathons or even ultramarathons.

Track training concentrates on speed rather than

endurance. The standard track is 400 meters, which is just under a quarter mile.

One of the benefits of going to the track is that there may be a couple of coaches there training their runners, and they (a coach or their runners) may not mind giving you tips. They may even welcome you to join a workout, which will allow you to try a practice session to decide what type of running suits you.

Winning...

Many runners aim to go for the gold. That is their vision, and they make it their exclusive mission. But for most runners, simply completing a half-marathon or a full marathon before the official cutoff time is their goal. It's the uniqueness of our lifestyles and choices that come into play here.

I know a guy who has run the Comrades ultramarathon in South Africa, a grueling race of 55 miles (89+ km), who keeps going back to do it "one more time!" The Comrades Marathon is the oldest and largest ultramarathon in the world. It was first run in 1921 and is known for its spirit of camaraderie.

...Or Just Racing

Many people simply enjoy the camaraderie of training and racing with others. The vibe on race day is something you have to experience to believe. It's exhiJeanneting, and it's all about sharing tips and motivating each other throughout the race. You meet different people from all walks of life and bond with them during the uphill stretches. The motivation and care from complete strangers, even though they are your competitors, are an eye-opener.

Many people enter races not to achieve the ultimate first prize but to achieve a personal goal and enjoy the camaraderie. Mark, another friend of mine, has run the Comrades Marathon 20 times, but for him, that is enough of a challenge. I've asked him whether he doesn't want to win as he gets a completion medal every year, but he told me the win for him is in completing the race, especially at his age (58).

There are racing events for everybody. Some seek the thrill of the competition, while others simply enjoy maintaining an average pace and are elated to cross the finish line.

Distance running can be for everyone. You will definitely find some distance to suit your fitness level and goal. They vary from 5K (3.1 miles) to half-marathons (13.1 miles) and full marathons (26.2 miles). There are even ultramarathons of 100 miles, 200 miles, or farther. So, something is bound to interest you.

Lock Your Eyes on Your Goal and Get Started!

Some uninformed people don't view adult runners as athletes or sports participants. Running is characterized as a mere way to blow off some stress and get good exercise. But runners, even those not engaged in competitive running, take their sport seriously.

Ultimate Decision Time

These are the steps you should take before embarking on serious training:

Medical Checkup

Always consult your medical professional, and have your heart, lung capacity, and blood pressure checked. You can't go from a full couch potato to a marathon runner in a month. Your health is important and adds to the joy and exhiJeannetion of running!

The Right Trainers

Running shoes are extremely important, and you need to invest in a good pair right from the start. Many specialty running stores employ staff who can advise you on the tread and the way the running shoe fits at the arch of the foot. All feet are not created equal, and designers of trainers and racing shoes have taken this into consideration when developing and advancing the technology of running shoes.

The Gear

Specialty running stores also have all the latest gear that makes your run a pleasure and not a chore. There are many types of sports apparel now that dry instantly, a new scientific breakthrough. Also, consider the environment where you run, as you may need anything from gloves to sunscreen in addition to standard running apparel.

Personal Care

It is important to be aware of your health and safety when you run. Taking care of your body is one of the main reasons why stretching is so important. To loosen up muscles after a good night's sleep or after sitting in an office chair all day, you can't simply get right into your running stride.

Do some warmup stretches and maybe a bit of walking just to warm up and loosen your muscles. You may even benefit from an easy jog for a couple of minutes before you increase your speed.

Something else to remember is to stay alert to your environment while running, especially if you are wearing earbuds to play your favorite music. You may be tempted to block out the world and go into a meditative state when it is just you, the road (or trail), and your music, but you need to be somewhat engaged with your surroundings to watch out for distracted drivers or people.

Newbies

If you have decided to run as exercise or for stress relief, consider starting your training using the run-walk method, which is especially popular among marathoners and ultramarathoners. Start out by walking (no running) for a couple of miles to assess whether the distance is too taxing.

Once you've done that, begin to add short running segments while gradually increasing the distance. You are now doing run-walk 'intervals,' which is a good way to build endurance. Many new runners find this method to be a good kickoff point. It also causes less strain on the joints.

Some runners adopt a routine of consistently alternating one minute of running with one minute of walking. Once they are comfortable with this and have built up some confidence, they systematically increase the run-walk ratio to 2:1, then 3:1, then 4:1, and so forth. Eventually, you can eliminate the walking break if it doesn't seem necessary anymore.

You are the Manager of Your Run

For most people who begin running as a way to get exercise, it's initially challenging, but as you get fitter and find your stride and your pace, you will begin to enjoy your runs more and more. When running, keep it relaxed, and don't overdo your first runs. It will just make you kick your trainers off and into the back of the closet, never to see the light of day again.

The whole idea is to relax and enjoy peaceful moments. Whenever you find yourself getting out of breath, try to do belly breathing while you run. Or, stop for a moment, take a couple of deep breaths, do some stretching, and then continue with your run.

In general, the way to breathe when you run is through your mouth. This will ensure your blood vessels, lungs, and heart get the maximum oxygen that can be used and keep you moving with little or no strain.

Don't forget the cooldown! You may think that you have used all your energy up on running, so you can screech to a halt and flop down on the couch. *Wrong!* Finish each run by slowing your pace to an easy jog or walk.

And there's more! After your run, you can do some stretches to further relax your muscles and promote your fitness.

Manage Your Form

Although running is an instinctual movement that your body is naturally capable of doing, that does not mean that you can simply run without thinking about *how* you are running.

Your running form should naturally improve over time, which will add to the efficiency of your running, but there are also things you can do to improve your form. Once you do, you might notice that proper form shaves off a few seconds or even minutes when it counts at races.

Proper form allows you to conserve energy, run farther and/or faster, and reduce injuries. What follows are some practical tips you can implement.

Manage Your Posture

Do you remember what your parents always told you about walking, standing, and sitting? It was to sit up straight, keep your head lifted, keep your shoulders back, stretch your back and keep it straight, walk tall, and don't forget to pull in your stomach.

The same basic principles apply to running.

Focus on these points: (a) Stand tall and straight. (b) Relax your shoulders and arms. (c) Keep your chest out. (d) Maintain a slight forward lean as it is gravitationally easier and allows your body to flow toward the next forward movement.

Another aspect of posture that long-distance runners must be aware of is the problem of shoulder rounding. As a runner gets tired, they tend to hunch their shoulders. Shoulders that are rounded forward affect the chest by not allowing the lungs enough capacity to expand when taking in a breath. While running, focus on a central point in the distance, which will prevent your shoulders from rounding.

While running, let your arms move naturally with your stride. If you are a trained runner, your arms should bend naturally at an angle of 90 degrees at the elbow. Keep your elbows close to your waist. Relax your hands and avoid clenching them as this will lead to neck and shoulder tension.

Don't stress too much about your form. Remember, running is fun! It is about the sport, the camaraderie, and the sheer enjoyment of physical exercise for your body, your mind, and your soul.

Manage Your Foot Strike

As unique individuals, we also have a unique way of walking and running. Some of us land in the middle of the foot while others land on their heels. Others land closer to their toes. The way that your foot hits the road is called a 'foot strike' in runner lingo.

If heel-toe or toe-heel is the way you naturally run, don't change it if it feels comfortable. Researchers have found that purposefully changing the foot strike of a runner has a detrimental effect on their natural style, so embrace your natural foot strike.

...And They're Off!

Now that the basics of running have been discussed, it's time to get moving.

Even if you aren't yet fit, you can build your stamina to a solid level by initially running for only 30 minutes, three days a week, for 10 weeks. For a newbie, it's better to start with a 10-week run-walk plan. Ten weeks might sound like a short time to you, but it's been confirmed that this timing plan works well even for people in different age groups who are starting from the 'couch.'

Make it your goal to start by running three days per week, and then use the alternate days to do some stretching and flexing exercises. Once again, it is important to remember that you are unique. Your body is unique, and while some people may recover quicker than you do, there is nothing wrong with your running.

Follow This Beginner Plan

- *Warming Up/ Cool Down:* Before you start running, it is important to warm up your muscles. Not only does this prevent injury, but it also sets your frame of mind. Start with a fast walk for five to ten minutes before you do any running. After running move into your cooldown for the last five to ten minutes by switching to a brisk walk and then a slower walk.

- *Ramping Up:* Your aim is to start by running three times a week, but if you only do two runs the first week due to post-run stiffness, relax, that's your body telling you what to do. Always listen to your body like a well-oiled machine. If it's running out of gas or oil, it will tell you.
- *Recovery Days:* You may think you are a superhero and can just hit the road and run. Unfortunately, that is not the case. Give your muscles time to recover between runs. Remember, you have only just started your training program.
- *Cross-Training:* On recovery days, you can go for a swim, play tennis with a friend, or go cycling. This will allow other muscle groups to get a workout and improve your overall health and fitness.
- *Find Your Sweet Spot:* Your ideal sweet spot is the place between comfort and discomfort, between laziness and ambition. That is...your *sweet* spot!

Week	Running Plan	Time
Week 1	1-minute run, 2-minute walk – repeat 7 x	21 Minutes
Week 2	2-minute run, 2-minute walk – repeat 5 x	20 Minutes
Week 3	3-minute run, 2-minute walk – repeat 4 x	20 minutes
Week 4	5-minute run, 2-minute walk – repeat 3 x	21 minutes
Week 5	6-minute run, 90 seconds walk – repeat 3 x	22 minutes
Week 6	8-minute run, 1-minute walk – repeat 3 x	27 minutes
Week 7	10-minute run, 1-minute walk – repeat 3 x	33 minutes
Week 8	13-minute run, 1-minute walk – repeat 2 x	28 minutes
Week 9	15-minute run, 1-minute walk – repeat 2 x	32 minutes
Week 10	30 minutes of continuous running	30 minutes
Week 11	Celebrate your achievement!	

Alter the plan to suit your fitness level and lifestyle. If you are generally fit from walking, then you should start by walking at a brisk pace for 30 minutes.

When embarking on this training plan, listen to your body. Your body will give you signs when you are overdoing it. Then simply dial back your training until you feel ready to move forward to the next stage. Even if it takes longer than 10 weeks, your goal is to become a runner, and you are essentially a born runner!

Manage Your Run

Intensity: Running at an easy to moderate pace that elevates your heart rate is where you want to focus. As a safety measure, however, periodically take the 'talk test': If you cannot say a sentence without gasping for breath, your pace may be too intense.

Manage Your Pace

Pace: When you are in the beginner's training phase, it is important to watch your pace. You should be doing slow, comfortable run-walks and runs. Don't start off your training at the fastest pace you can manage. Your pace should be faster than a fast walk but not too much faster at first. This is not the time to be focusing on your pace alone. Pace can be a greater focus as you get fitter.

Manage Your Intervals

Intervals: Whether you are doing run-walk intervals as a beginner or track intervals (alternating fast segments with jogged segments) as a seasoned competitor, intervals are integral to building your fitness. You are likely training to be a long-distance runner, not a sprinter. This means managing all the factors of your run, so look at intervals as a holistic method of training. If you manage every facet of your run, you will ensure your recovery rate is good, so you are building a holistic level of fitness. Managing your runs will help you maintain form, stride, and strength—the perfect recipe for eventually building up to doing a marathon!

Chapter 5
Eat, Drink and Repeat

"To eat is a necessity, but to eat intelligently is an art."
— La Rochefoucauld

Optimum Nutrition is Needed to Fuel Your Body

The nutrients our body requires to function optimally have a direct impact on memory, mood, and mental focus. Scientific research has shown that nutrition plays a large role in mental health and cognitive functioning. This research confirmed the brain-gut connection and demonstrated that maintaining a healthy gut with good foods that are high in antioxidants and filled with omega-3, vitamins, and minerals ensure physical energy, mental focus, and high attention.

What is Optimum Nutrition?

It is getting the right nutrients to the right cells at the right time. A holistic diet filled with the nutrients essential to create energy and meet the demands of training is the primary focus. Essential nutrients not only supply enough energy to cells but also aid during the rest and recovery phase, regenerating cells that have been active during training.

An athlete requires a diet that takes into consideration their personal needs and the needs of their specific activity. This diet should focus on the following requirements:

- Calorific Needs
- Macronutrients
- Meal and Snack Timing
- Vitamins and Minerals
- Hydration

Nutrition Essentials for Runners

Athletes need to plan their nutritional requirements according to their sport type. It seems, however, that when it comes to running, there are many opinions on what is best. For a runner, the essential elements are to fuel and recover using an optimal nutrition plan.

Our bodies are unique and perform intricate biological processes that ensure our cells are fueled to survive and move in synergy, so fueling your body is not as simple as energy in = energy out. Finding out what your specific nutritional requirements are is a process of eliminating foods one by one that you think might not agree with your body. As you eliminate foods, make notes on the effects they have on your body and modify your diet to exclude foods that are disagreeable for your needs.

Making the right choices when it comes to your nutrition, lifestyle, and training will provide you with the energy you need to stay motivated, train day after day, and perform at your peak. These are the micro-elements that will ultimately bring improvement for you to enjoy your challenges and reap the rewards of success.

Manage your Nutrition

Curious Carbohydrates

Carbohydrates are critical in providing a fuel source for athletes and training. Carbs are broken down into glucose, which is the main fuel source for cells. When your body does not need to use glucose for energy, it is stored as glycogen in the liver and muscles. The glycogen stored in the muscles is most readily available when an energy boost is required; marathon runners will find this form of energy storage is limited and inadequate for their use. This proves how vital it is to ensure your carb intake is planned and supplied with the right type of carbohydrates for training or during marathons. Your glycogen stores require around 500 grams of carbs to reach maximum capacity. This means your fuel tank is full.

Fuel Fact

If you are training on most days, you need to ensure that you never reach a carbohydrate-depleted state. This means that after training sessions, you must ensure you get the correct nutrients to replenish and regenerate your cells. Keeping your cells healthy and active will maximize your running performance and ensure that your overall health is in premium condition to enjoy many years of training and racing.

Fueling Up

Filling your fuel tank for a marathon requires some planning for timed-release energy. Plan for 1g of carb intake for every 1kg of body weight per hour (2.2 lbs). This ratio is highly dependent on your personal needs, so try to perfect your intake and use during training. Carry a sports drink, gel, or snack bar in a sports pack on your run.

Glucose and fructose are good in-run fuels as the body readily absorbs around 60 grams of glucose and 30 grams of fructose per hour depending on the size and frame of the athlete. Studies show that males with a larger frame can easily consume 90 to 120 grams per hour. Another factor to consider is the altitude at which you are running as this too affects consumption.

Remember to fuel:

1. Within the first 30 to 45 minutes after the race starts, you should have taken in enough fuel to supply sufficient glucose. Then top up your fuel tank every 30 to 45 minutes.
2. Consume enough liquids to ensure better digestion. Your basic rule of thumb here is that 1g carb requires 10ml of water.
3. Replace fluids gradually, ensuring that your fluids contain enough sodium and electrolytes to replenish your cells. Your body loses 400ml to 800ml per hour depending on perspiration loss, the weather, and the altitude. Make sure you rehydrate before, during, and after the run.

Perfect Proteins

Proteins are known as the building blocks of the body and contain amino acids, which are seen as the most important macronutrient for optimum nutrition. The body is made up of 20 different amino acids that are combined in different sequences and found in muscles, bones, skin, tendons, hair, and other tissue. Eight essential amino acids must be included in your daily nutritional intake to transport nutrients and produce enzymes. These are found in animal protein such as beef, fish, chicken, eggs, and dairy products. Other sources of protein can be found in vegetables and grains, but they need to be combined with other sources to be a complete protein source.

Protein is an important macronutrient that aids cells during the recovery phase after training sessions. Protein in the muscle is broken down during resistance training and endurance sports such as long-distance running, cycling, and swimming.

Foods rich in protein should be eaten throughout the day to ensure constant cell recovery.

Fat Facts

All fats are not created equal, and fat does not make fat. These are myths that we have heard in the media and on social media that support the crazy diet industry and the sales of products for the financial gain of corporations. The bottom line is that fats are essential for the absorption of the fat-soluble vitamins A, D, E, and K. These essential fatty acids are required for cell recovery and prevent fatigue and inflammation. These vitamins are immune-boosting and have a high energy value.

Avoid saturated fats such as pies, cakes, biscuits, bacon fat, fatty meat, and sausage, and bulk up on good fats found in avocadoes, oily fish (mackerel and salmon), olive oil, and nuts. It is important to avoid trans fats, the fat found in some processed foods.

Vitamin and Mineral Essentials

Keeping your body functioning at optimum capacity requires micronutrients that function as coenzymes and aid the metabolic processing of proteins. To metabolize carbohydrates and fat, the B vitamins are essential. For immune-boosting, vitamins C and zinc are important, and magnesium and calcium are vital for muscles and bone density.

Runners need to ensure they fill up with micronutrients for general health and to be in peak running condition.

Focus on getting enough of the following:

Vitamins: A, B, C, D, E, and K
Minerals: Calcium, iron, and phosphorous
Electrolytes: Sodium and potassium
Trace elements: Magnesium, iodine, and zinc

To Supplement or Not to Supplement

There are many supplements out there that promise the world: energy-filled days, a memory like Albert Einstein, and even immortality in the case of anti-aging pills. But how much of this is real? The research has been inconclusive, but the key is that your daily diet is well-balanced. If you are eating nutrient-rich meat, fish, dairy, vegetables, and grains, you are getting all the vitamins and minerals you need. Yes, free radicals and pesticides used on the vegetables we eat might present a case for the use of supplements, but again, if your diet is well-balanced, you will meet your RDA (Recommended Daily Allowance) of vitamins and minerals.

Hydration

Hydration and taking in electrolytes are important in endurance running, and it's not only about fluid intake. It also relates to the thermoregulation of the body. During endurance running such as in a marathon, adequate hydration ensures there is adequate blood volume. Plasma regulation and volume have a direct impact on an athlete's performance. When your core temperature rises, you are at risk of dehydration resulting in a reduction of plasma (blood) volume. Loss of plasma volume leads to impaired cognitive function, an elevated heart rate, and fatigue. The best cure is prevention—so hydrate!

How Much to Hydrate?

First, measure your sweat. When determining your hydration requirements, you need to look at the distance you will be running, how long you will be running, the terrain on which you will be running, and your sweat rate. This will give you an indication of how much to hydrate. The best way to measure fluid loss is to weigh yourself before and after the run, so make a note to do that.

Pre-Run Hydration

Don't gulp down massive amounts of water or sports drinks five minutes before a race (or any run). As you may have already learned firsthand, this will impair your running and lead to cramps, making all your weeks of training null and void. Fluids should be consumed before you run, but take care not to consume too much as this will result in the liquids 'sloshing' about in your stomach while you run.

On-the-Run Hydration

Maintaining your fluid level while running is an important factor that affects thermoregulation and plasma volume, which in turn regulates your heartbeat, blood pressure, blood sugar, and cognitive functioning (decision-making). Drink fluids at regular intervals, taking into consideration perspiration loss, weather, terrain, altitude, and your pace.

During the race, you can begin by taking in 0.4 to 0.8 liters per hour depending on your weight and pace. Faster, heavier runners in a warm climate can start at 0.8 liters, while smaller runners in a cooler climate who run at a slower pace can begin at 0.4 liters. Use a sports drink that contains electrolytes and carbs. This combination of carbs and electrolytes maintains exercise performance.

Post-Run Hydration

You are elated. You have crossed the finish line! But don't let this thrill stop you from hydrating. Replacing fluids after a run is vital. If you feel you are dehydrated, drink as much fluid as you need to satisfy your thirst. But do not over-hydrate as this can lead to hyponatremia. Most trained runners can simply eat and drink normally to allow their bodies to replenish lost nutrients and fluids.

The Runner's Plate

Design your personalized menu with a focus on these foods:

Carbohydrates

Carbs are the best source of energy. To determine your training or marathon racing requirements, factor in the intensity that you are running to work out the carbs ratio that is best for your body type.

The human body functions efficiently on carbs as long as they are unprocessed, such as whole-grain foods. Whole-grain rice, pasta, and bread provide essential nutrients that include the B vitamins (folate, niacin, thiamine), zinc, iron, magnesium, and manganese. These high-fiber foods will satisfy your hunger pangs and are delicious and nutritious when paired with the right proteins and fats:

- Whole-grain bread
- Whole-grain rice
- Whole-grain pasta
- Potatoes
- Starchy vegetables
- Fruits

Protein

Protein provides essential nutrients to repair and regenerate cells. This is an important bodily function after training or racing. Protein should make up 10% to 35% of your caloric intake, which depends on your frame. For female athletes, it is best to consume 25g to 30g of protein high in leucine within 30 to 45 minutes after exercise, according to Stacy Sims in her book, *Roar: How to Match Your Food and Fitness to your Unique Female Physiology for Optimum Performance, Great Health, and a Strong, Lean Body for Life.*

Runners need to work out their best ratio as each athlete is unique and requires a different amount of protein for every pound of weight. When consuming proteins, keep an eye on the fat content to avoid cholesterol issues. Here are some examples of protein sources:

- Lean meat
- Fish
- Chicken
- Eggs
- Beans
- Dairy
- Whole grains

Fats

Eat foods low in cholesterol and saturated fats so that they only account for about 20% to 30% of your diet. Include these delicious foods in your diet to be sure you are living a healthy, energized life:

- Avocados
- Nuts (almonds, pecans, Brazil nuts, hazelnuts, walnuts)
- Coldwater fish (salmon, mackerel, herring, tuna)
- Olive oil and canola oil
- Seeds (chia, flax)

Forget Fast Foods

Athletes limit or avoid some foods. Consider that the body doesn't crave these foods when nutritional requirements are met with healthy, delicious, and nutritious foods. Limit the following foods:

Fast Food: Burgers, French fries, fried chicken, donuts
Processed Meats: Deli meats, salami, pepperoni, sausages
Unhealthy Fats: Lard, bacon fat, cream, margarine, trans fats
Sugary Foods: Jam, pudding, frosting, condiments, sauces

Time Your Bite

Timing is critical when it comes to nutrition. Athletes know what to eat to ensure they get enough carbs, proteins, fats, vitamins, and minerals. They also understand that timing is a major factor when running. Eating the right foods at the right time ensures energy levels are high while training, and energy levels post-exercise are also important. Try different foods and snacks to establish what gives you the best source of timed-release energy. Eat at least an hour before you train or run to ensure your body has completely digested your meal.

How Far?

Glycogen stores are the fuel stores needed by the body for energy. Taking in sufficient carbohydrates ensures a timed release for runners. A well-balanced diet that includes good carbs will maintain adequate storage of glycogen in the muscles and liver. Your body accesses the glycogen stored in the muscles first and then moves to the glycogen stored in the liver.

Pre-Run Nutrition

Runners who run for less than one hour can consider a carb-rich snack such as:

- Banana
- Medjool dates
- Smoothie with fruit and yogurt
- Scrambled eggs and whole-grain toast
- Peanut butter on a bagel
- Self-baked oat muffins or cookies

Carb-Loading

The term 'carb-loading' refers to loading up on carbohydrate-rich foods and snacks before a long run or race. Complex carbohydrates should be eaten a few days before running a marathon or taking part in an event that will last at least 90 minutes. These carbs are broken down by the body and stored in the muscles as glycogen for access when needed. Carb-loading requires 3.5 to 4.5 grams of carbs per pound of body mass.

During Your Long Run

For the first 30 to 45 minutes of running, you are accessing the glycogen stores in your muscles for energy. After that, your body uses glucose from your reserves, so you should eat a carb-rich snack. As an athlete, you know you need to replenish your glucose. Enjoy a flavorful gel pouch so you have enough energy to reach the finish line.

Choose a carb-rich snack from these healthy options:

- Banana
- Crackers or pretzels
- Energy bar (test it!)
- Energy gel (test it!)

Top Tip

Test your nutrition plan for long-distance running before you put it into action. Start with small bites as you will need to train your stomach. While running, your body is busy making sure that all of its functions are performing well, so naturally, it might not have your stomach as a priority. Digestion issues are therefore a common result. Energy gels and bars are highly concentrated. They look small and innocent, but believe me, they are a full load in an untrained stomach. Also, keep in mind that what you eat should reflect your lifestyle and values. You don't want to be all about health and then in training and racing take whatever is handed to you. Remember, you are in this for the long run!

Post-Run

Elation! You've made it across the finish line! You've achieved your goal! This is what you were training for, and nothing feels this good!

The time has come to replenish your nutrients. If you feel like a hamburger and french fries, now is the time to enjoy one! This is the time to break the rules and enjoy something totally off your nutritional menu. If it's a waffle with ice cream, that's okay; you've earned your calories!

Some people don't feel hungry after a run, but the bottom line is that you have to replenish the vitamins and minerals you lost while running. Try to at least have a light carb-protein snack.

These are some delicious options:

- Whole-wheat pasta with meat sauce
- Peanut butter and banana on whole-wheat bread
- Eggs on toast
- Smoothie or protein shake

R & R time! Replenish and regenerate your stressed muscles.

Short and Sweet

Be Sure to Eat Enough

Yes, you want to get fit and fab and run the marathon of your dreams. The problem is that you are continuously hungry. This means you aren't eating enough. Go through your meal plan and bulk up on a variety of delicious foods. You know what you enjoy eating; this is a lifestyle, not a *diet*. Live your life and eat enough.

Hydrate Properly

Hydrate with H2O; nothing tastes as good as crystal-clear water. Enjoy a glass of H2O straight or mixed with some fruit juice. Always make sure you are well-hydrated because, after all, our bodies are 70% water.

Replenish Electrolytes

Running for one hour or more draws down your potassium and sodium stores, so it's time to refuel your cells. There are some delicious foods, beverages, and flavors you can choose from to replenish your electrolytes.

Limit Fiber and FODMAP Before You Race

Fermentable oligosaccharides, disaccharides, monosaccharides, and polyols, oh my! Yes, it's a mouthful, but to optimize your nutritional intake, you must include FODMAPS. Limit your FODMAP intake, however, when preparing for a marathon. They can cause digestive discomfort. Foods low in FODMAPS are:

- Meat and eggs
- Cheddar, feta, and brie cheese
- Grains (oats, rice, quinoa)
- Almond milk

Be sure to keep meals small but satisfying before a race

Practice on Long Runs

When you are preparing for a marathon or other long-distance run or race, adjust your meal plan according to your nutritional and energy needs. Try carbs for a timed release when training. You know your nutritional needs for energy, vitamins, and minerals. Try different foods if you wish, and adjust the timing to suit your needs.

Top Tip

Think like a pro by using your long runs as rehearsals for race day. Prepare the exact food you plan to eat the day before, have the same breakfast, and practice your race nutrition. This gives you time to adjust and adds confidence.

Listen to Your Body

We are unique beings with unique needs, so listen to your body as it will give you indications of what you are lacking nutritionally. Base your meal plans on foods you enjoy eating and limit the foods you don't like. Have fun pairing new combinations. Have you ever had a PB & banana sandwich? It creates a taste sensation in your mouth.

Chapter 6

Recovery is Underrated but Important

"You have brains in your head. You have feet in your shoes. You can steer yourself in any direction you choose." — Dr. Seuss

Runners are well-trained athletes who know they may face injuries. There is no question that their training and preparation for races include a thorough knowledge and preparation for the pitfalls of injuries and how to avoid them.

Prevent Pain

Runners understand the impact of each foot strike and know it can take a toll on the body, but they also know how to swing the odds in their favor. Here are six methods to turn the odds in *your* favor to avoid running injuries.

Footwear Facts

Wearing the right running shoes is essential. Not only will wearing the correct trainers give your self-confidence a boost, but properly designed footwear takes into consideration the arch of the foot, the shape of the foot, and toe shapes and sizes. Using a treadmill and camera, many running stores offer gait analysis to help them put you in the right shoes for your feet. After a short treadmill run in the pair of shoes you are thinking of purchasing, you can watch a playback of your run. The biggest factor in choosing a shoe is to determine how much you pronate, which can be gleaned from gait analysis. Pronation refers to the way the foot rolls into each foot strike and how the angle corresponds with the lower leg.

The running shoe you select should be snug but with some wiggle room for your toes. Specialty running stores will do a proper fitting and advise you on which trainer to choose. Take your running socks with you for fittings to ensure you get a comfortable trainer that fits with your socks on. If you wear a sports bra, take that with you too as it may affect your posture as you run.

Footwear Maintenance

Trainers need to be replaced every 300 to 500 miles, or around six months for regular runners. There are different schools of thought regarding which types of trainers are best, from beefy shoes to no shoes at all (yes, barefoot running is a thing). Companies want to offer you the best innovations, but they also want to sell. Do your research and decide what makes sense for you. Just ensure you allow time for the transition; you don't want to train for six months in Stone Age trainers and then lace up your new shiny ones on the marathon. Blister city!

Muscle Flexing

Flexing and stretching your muscles keeps them loose and limber. Keeping your body loose and supple like a well-oiled machine improves performance, and the increased range of motion enhances your balance in addition to your flexibility. Mentally, it leaves you calm and focused. Yoga is an extraordinary tool to create balance and flexibility and find inner calmness, allowing you to mentally focus on the marathon training at hand.

Gym Bodies

Endurance runners can reap huge benefits from strength training as it increases muscle strength, endurance, and bone density. Schedule at least two weekly gym days, work with weights, and watch your muscles develop that toned, sculpted look. Looking good is not the only benefit as stronger muscles are less likely to be injured and allow you to finish runs and races strong by maintaining good posture.

Your Body Knows Best

Tuning into your body is one of the best ways to determine what your body requires. This includes rest and nutritional needs. Even when you have a perfect training plan, your body may sometimes feel sluggish and rundown, so listen to your body. Your body may be telling you it's time to reevaluate and rest. Rest is critical to recovery and cell regeneration. Don't push your body past its limits. Listen to it. Pushing your body may lead to dangerous fatigue and injuries, and your mind will not be on your run. If you are a lady, lucky you! You have a monthly reminder that your body is on track. Especially when you're training, make note of your menstruation cycle.

Gradual is Best

Yes, you are a runner, but it is not one of those activities where you jump into the water and automatically swim. Endurance running and building strength must be done over a period of time. If you are training for a 5K run, don't even think of completing the distance after one week of training. Launch your training with the Beginner Plan in Chapter Four. Start with walks and run-walks, and increase the distances regularly and *gradually*.

Top Tip

Never increase your distance and intensity during the same week. This is too taxing on your physical and mental strength. A good way to increase your training is to add increments of 10% per week.

Medical Advice

Before embarking on a lifestyle change such as a running program, visit your doctor. Consider full blood work to determine whether your body is sufficiently healthy and meeting all of its vitamins and mineral requirements. This visit will also establish a baseline for your regular checkups. As a runner, these regular checkups will give you an indication of what nutrients and vitamins you must increase in your daily eating plan. The doctor will be able to compare your current results with your baseline results and tell you if you are lacking any vitamins or minerals. This is when you can consider supplements or changes in your diet. Be sure your doctor checks your muscle mass and body fat along with your blood work.

Some R & R

Rest and recovery are as important as training and racing. Your cells constantly need to recover from runs. Cells are the building blocks of the human body and give structure to the body in the form of red and white blood cells, bone cells, and skin cells. Each cell type has a specific function, and allowing each cell to recover and be replenished requires nutrients found in the food we eat.

Listen to Your Body

Rest days are essential for most runners. In the runner's world, however, even the word 'rest' is often deemed unacceptable. Some runners believe they will lose their endurance and speed if they rest, even if it's only for one day.

The bottom line is that rest and recovery are as important as training and have some unbelievable benefits. Put on the kettle, put your feet up, and read the scientifically-backed reasons for rest days. Know that even the world's top runners incorporate rest days into their schedules.

Take a Rest

Scientific research has shown that rest days benefit runners in the following ways:

- **Reduced Risk of Injury**

Following a good running schedule that includes rest and recovery avoids micro-damage to muscles and cells. During planned rest periods, your muscles and cells have time to repair and regrow damaged tissue. Planned rest days will avoid overexerting and overusing muscles and reduce injuries such as tendonitis, stress fractures, and shin splints.

- **Increased Fitness Level**

This doesn't make sense, right? Wrong! Your body's fitness level improves while you rest. As your body recovers during a rest period, your cells are given time to recover and repair. Your body adapts physiologically when you remain static. That is not to suggest that you slouch on the couch all day! Do some gentle stretching, or take a restful walk.

- **Mental Recharge**

Planned rest days allow for a mental recharge. Similar to rechargeable batteries, your mind needs to regularly recharge. The constant stress of training, especially before a marathon, takes a toll on the mind. Similar to a Fortune 500 company CEO who suffers from burnout due to overwork, you need rest days to avoid burnout due to overtraining.

- **Increased Training Capability**

When you allow your body adequate time to rest, you will find that after a recovery period, you will be able to train longer and harder. Your body has become fine-tuned as your cells are prepared to train again.

- **Consistent Training Energy**

Training consistently is a good goal for any runner. By ensuring you have planned recovery periods in your training schedule, you will avoid overtraining fatigue. Consistent training and recovery sessions will build endurance. This is safer and more realistic than training for hours on end, leading to muscle (and mental) fatigue that may even make you want to skip your scheduled training sessions altogether.

- **Peak Race-Day Performance**

Real physical fitness is gained through weeks and weeks of training, not by training long and hard day after day. To maximize performance, you need to follow your training plan, which should be followed by a tapering plan to get you race-ready. This will give you the confidence to rest during the week before your marathon or other race.

You will know you have done the planning and followed your schedule. Now you are ready for the big day!

- **Periodized Training**

Being in peak physical shape all year long isn't possible or even desirable. Consider dividing your year into periods of training and recovery. Break the year into quarters, for example, and take it three months at a time. Now decide what area to focus on during each quarter of the year. For example, focus on your strength in the first quarter, on your stamina in the second quarter, and so on. This will give you the challenge and variety to keep training throughout the year as you will have to focus on perfecting each aspect of running.

Break your year into smaller cycles, called 'mesocycles.' For example, if you decide to train for a marathon over the course of eight months and are generally fit, adjust your plan based on your main goal—your 'A' race. You can start off with a focus on strength training for the first couple of months and then take the strength into your run later on. Also consider some test races, which we'll call 'B' and 'C' races. These events should come close to imitating your 'A' race and give you time to adjust your training plan. A great 'B' race can be a half-marathon; a 'C' race can be a 10K.

Body Signals

Your scheduled training program is your guide, but don't let it be your sole guide. Listen to your body. Pay attention to what your body is telling you, and adapt your training and rest periods accordingly. It could be that you had a rest day planned, yet you feel like running; then do it. Alternatively, you might have a scheduled training session planned but your headspace is not focused. Substitute a bike ride, a walk or simply reading a book. The next day, when your head and body are aligned, resume your schedule.

Six Slow-Down Factors

These are areas to pay attention to while training:

Constant Pain in Muscles or Joints

Having sore muscles as an athlete is normal, especially if you recently increased your endurance or strength training. This type of pain usually goes away after a couple of days. If the pain persists longer than this or gets worse, however, it may precede or indicate an injury. Running can cause your calves and hamstrings to feel slightly sore, but you need to ensure the soreness doesn't persist.

Do some stretching to relax these muscles, and if the pain persists, it's time to stop running for a while and see a sports-medicine specialist (such as an orthopedist or podiatrist) or physical therapist. Pain that lasts longer than three days in any muscle group is a sign to slow down and get a checkup if it continues.

Sleep Deprivation

Healthy sleep cycles last between seven and nine hours per night. If you are feeling tired most days, it's time to examine your sleep patterns. For a runner, good sleep is essential. This is the time when your cells regrow and repair. When you go to sleep, they get to work!

Here again, the advice is the same: Listen to your body. If you've spent all night tossing and turning and scheduled a training run after breakfast, cancel the run and catch some morning zzz's.

Elevated Resting Heart Rate

Your health is optimal, and you are fit and fab, yet your heart rate seems to be sending a signal that something is not right. Listen to your heart. No, it's not Valentine's Day this time; it's your heart telling you there is a possible issue with your cardiovascular health. Heed the warning; see your doctor. Your body may be fighting something.

Feeling Stressed Out

Even serious runners have lives. Maybe it's a busy schedule at work, a new job, children to take to school and to help with homework, or household chores. You are pushed to the max. Your mind is constantly occupied with making lists of what must be done: to-do lists, shopping lists, training schedules... There are simply not enough hours in a day.

Adapt or cry? Just take it slowly. Instead of going for your three-hour training run, opt for an easier run. Try a new route, admire the architecture of the surrounding buildings, or if you are lucky enough to run through a park, take a breather to stretch at a bench while watching the world hurry by. Remind yourself that the people passing by also only have 24 hours in a day, and their lives might be as busy as yours. The fact is, you are not alone in this, and tomorrow is another day to train, so be content to relax today.

Your Progress has Stagnated

Your planned schedule for training has seemingly been going well. If you are following your carefully planned schedule and it's Week 5, you might be expecting that you can improve your times and not feel tired after running your standard routes. But after completing your first run of the week, you are disappointed to see that your time is a bit slower than the previous week.

Maybe you are just having an 'off' day, so check your time on that week's next run. If you find there is still no improvement, or your run seems extra difficult, it's time to analyze your two runs and your training schedule.

Spend some time scrutinizing all of the relevant data, starting with your pulse, your blood pressure, and your heart rate. Now consider your mental status. Are you feeling anxious, irritated, or moody? Are you getting enough sleep?

Your slower times may be the result of overtraining. Adjust your schedule, allocate extra rest days, and possibly alternate a run with a mind-body exercise like yoga or Pilates. Once your energy returns, you can rework your training schedule.

You Don't Feel Yourself

Your body is unique; your nutritional requirements are unique; and your training and fitness should be planned to suit your personal needs. Every person's *normal* is different; what is normal for me could be totally different from your normal. Keep an eye on any physiological changes. Are you getting headaches? Are you feeling ill or experiencing unexplained pains? These are indications that you should change some elements of your lifestyle. Optimize your training by ensuring that your nutritional needs are being met, you're getting enough sleep, your rest days are sufficient, and you're not overworking or overtraining.

"It's better to show up at the start line undertrained than overtrained," says Rahaf Khatib, an RRCA-certified run coach based in Farmington Hills, Michigan.

R & R & R & R & R & R & R

Be sure to get enough R's: Rest, Repair, Recharge, Regrow, Replenish, Recover, and (only then), Run. This doesn't mean you can lounge around and do nothing. Keep your body moving and your mind active.

These are important elements for holistic healthy living. But keep your body moving by trying some different activities:

- Do low-impact exercise.
- Shoot some hoops.
- Play games.
- Get quality sleep.
- Meditate.
- Strength-train.
- Do yoga.
- Swim.
- Take a Pilates class.

When planning your schedule, including your day-to-day life, you will notice that there is much to do in 24 hours. You might stop in your tracks when you see the word 'rest,' but that is one of the most important aspects of your training. Rest periods are as important as the training and the marathon. This is a 'timeout' for your body. Rest days strengthen your mind, body, and spirit. Resting cells recover and repair quickly; they also sharpen your cognitive processes. Meanwhile, you might feel that something is missing in your day—ah, the run!

While running, your body is using stored energy for fuel. This means that similar to a car's engine that needs a tune-up, your body needs one. After a marathon, your body has used all the glycogen stored in your muscles and liver. Now that you have reached your goal, it's time to turn your focus toward tissue repair and regrowth. It's time to make post-race care the center of attention.

According to Dr. Adam Tenforde, assistant professor of physical medicine and rehabilitation at Harvard University, "As much as athletes focus on their volume of training and the speed at which they do workouts, what they do outside of running is equally important to becoming stronger and more resilient in the future."

Dr. Bonnie Marks, a New York University Sports Performance Center staff psychologist, points out, "If you don't have time to recharge, it can lead to staleness and general apathy about your training."

Studies conducted at various sports-medicine centers found that rest and repair should be optimized. Take stock of your physical body before and after a rest day. You should feel motivated and energized to get back to running. Tweak your training and rest days, and notice how your body automatically seems stronger. Enjoying your rest day will give you time to miss your training, and you will be excited to hit the track, trail or road.

Regular Rest is Crucial

As an athlete, you know that rest is important. Ignore those who say, "So, why aren't you running today?" Or, "Are you tired?" Such myriad questions from non-athletes who don't understand! The fact is that trying to explain the cellular functions of repair and regrowth during rest will simply not figure as important knowledge in their cognitive processes, so you will be wasting your time.

Rest days are the days that your cells supply the nutrients to your body's biological processes, says Dr. Tenforde.

If you've still got ants in your 'runderpants', here are some more reasons to chillax:

No Stress Fractures

Runners know that bones benefit from running. With every foot strike, you are strengthening your bone tissue and cell-repair functioning. Your body needs 36 to 48 hours to recover on the bone/cellular level. These new cells are comprised of stronger structures. However, if you run without resting, these cells don't have sufficient time to repair. This is how a stress fracture begins.

Bounce-Back Buff

While running you are continuously strengthening your muscle groups. Running and other forms of exercise create microscopic tears in the muscle fibers. The natural response of the body is to repair and rebuild, making the new structure of the muscle stronger than the previous one. However, there is a catch. You need to take time off from training for the cells to jump into action and complete their task. Not taking enough time off for cell repair will cause additional damage as the process has not been completed.

Brain Chill

People run for different reasons, but for most people, running goes hand in hand with clearing out the cobwebs in the mind. Take note when you run: What is going on in your mind? Physiologically, your body is secreting cortisol hormones as it can't tell the difference between a fight-or-flight run and a run for the pure enjoyment and relaxation it brings. An increase in your cortisol levels can lead to disturbed sleep, mood issues, and irritability. Running usually has the opposite effect—longer, deeper sleep; improved mood; less stress. But the negatives stated previously can happen occasionally, especially for evening runners.

Take it Easy

Runners often debate over how much their fitness and strength levels are affected when they take a break. StrengthRunning.com cofounder Jason Fitzgerald says that scientific research has shown that you can rest for a full week without a decrease in your fitness level or your muscle mass and strength. Sports physicians suggest at least a one-to-two-week respite after a major endurance event.

Tight Tendons

Tendons are structures made from connective tissue and function as an attachment between the muscle and the bone. As your blood plasma moves through your veins and arteries, the tendons are unfortunately the last customer to be served. Tendons also take longer to repair and need a good supply of plasma-rich blood. Taking off enough time to repair the tendons requires a change in your training schedule.

Ensure that you give tendons enough time to repair after an injury. Tendons require anywhere from six weeks to six months to heal, depending on the injury sustained and its severity. Overuse of tendons leads to chronic damage, and the result is tendinitis—inflammation from constant foot-strike impact without allowing sufficient rest time.

Fine-Tuning

Just as a Steinway piano requires tuning by a master, your body needs fine-tuning. Fitzgerald says that if you allocate enough rest time, your cells will naturally repair themselves and heal instead of becoming a spot in your body where you are prone to becoming repeatedly injured.

To Serve and Protect

Your body takes its cues from your consciousness, and if you don't take scheduled rest days, its systems will constantly be on high alert. That means your inflammatory processes won't have time to shut down and rest. You are living in a state of constant overdrive, which can lead to issues with your immune system and susceptibility to infections and other illnesses. Kaye Edwards, an orthopedic specialist for Atlanta-based Precision Performance, found in her experience and research that taking at least one day off from activity reduces inflammation and gives your body time to repair.

The Recovery Run

Some seasoned runners do recovery runs as they find it beneficial to keep moving at a slower, less intense pace rather than reading a book or going for a walk. Recovery runs need to be easy on your body and mind, with no time pressure and no focus on stride or foot strike. They are simply relaxing runs where you can allow your mind to wander or enjoy being in nature. Running at a slow pace without putting pressure on your body and mind is one of the best ways to remain on the same fitness level.

Chapter 7
Pour in Your Soul

"You are no richer than what you carry in your mind, no stronger than what you hold in your heart, and no purer than what you harbor in your soul."
— Matshona Dhliwayo

Sincerely Scientific

Gratitude is not simply a matter of being grateful. What was always thought to be 'airy-fairy' has now been scientifically proven.

The term 'An Attitude of Gratitude' has been around for centuries. In fact, scholars believe that it stems from Saint Francis of Assisi's wise words, "For it is in giving that we receive."

An extensive study was undertaken by two professors at Indiana University. Joshua Brown, Ph.D., specializes in psychological and brain sciences. Joel Wong, Ph.D., is an associate professor of psychological counseling.

Most of the 300 participants in the study were college students who wanted psychological help. Most of them stated that they had issues with anxiety and depression.

The study divided the participants into three groups. Group 1 was asked to write one gratitude letter a week to another person for three weeks. Group 2 was asked to write about their innermost thoughts and feelings about negative experiences. Group 3 was not asked to do any writing of gratitude letters.

Group 1 showed an improvement in mental issues within four weeks. Twelve weeks after the study, the participants' emotions and attitudes of gratitude were still present.

The scientific tool used in the study was an fMRI scan that confirmed more activity in the prefrontal cortex when subjects experienced gratitude. The fMRI scans were done before the study began, then at four weeks, and again at 12 weeks. It was found that after 12 weeks, the brain was still indicating a positive attitude toward every aspect of life.

In contrast, the group writing about negative experiences or only receiving counseling did not show the same changes in the prefrontal cortex. These results suggest that practicing gratitude regularly has a lasting effect on the brain and could improve mental health in the future when practiced regularly.

U.C. Davis psychologist Robert Emmons's study showed that keeping a gratitude journal and writing about any experiences we are grateful for significantly increases well-being and general satisfaction in all areas of life.

The benefits of practicing an attitude of gratitude are endless and include a general feeling of happiness, more restful sleep patterns, more energy, and a sense of being in tune with life.

Graceful Gratitude

Little moments can bring a smile to your face and brighten up your day. Holding the elevator door for someone, seeing a flower in bloom, hearing laughter—these moments are special and can bring positivity into your life.

Gratitude in Practice

Journaling about your daily blessings and things you've enjoyed during the day—even people in your life who bring you joy—can be written in your journal.

Be grateful for your current situation, remember the hard times, and acknowledge how far you have come. Be grateful for the challenges you have been through and what you have learned.

Share your gratitude with colleagues, friends, and family. Research has confirmed that sharing gratitude strengthens relationships. When someone does something for you, show your gratitude. Gratitude is infectious.

Use your senses. Smell, taste, touch, hear, and see the beauty around you. Appreciate your experiences in life with gratitude.

Go through the motions—smile, say "thank you," and practice grateful motions to activate your attitude of gratitude.

People who are grateful use positive language and focus on the good in others and in life. They feel blessed and fortunate, and they want to share their gratitude.

Grateful Runners Lead the Pack

These leaders of the pack know their nutritional requirements, their recovery time, and so much more. Their knowledge is science-based.

Practicing physical health is foremost on their minds, so mental health comes naturally. The mind plays an integral part in training and racing. At times, athletes perfect their running in the months before race day, yet on the day, they may be unable to put their training into practice.

The focus of a runner plays an important role while racing, but they must be able to train their mind to overcome possible barriers such as insecurity or a fear of not completing the race. This, however, can be rectified by cultivating an attitude of gratitude. As you list the things you are grateful for, your confidence is boosted. You feel positive about the outcome. And why shouldn't you? You've got this, right?

Practice gratitude daily by incorporating it into your training, and be thankful as your run. There is so much to be thankful for. We can run, we have the gear, we have the energy and the stamina. Observe how gratitude attracts positive energy and creates a physical change.

Studies have shown that practicing gratitude reduces stress by 28%. Inflammation is reduced by more than 7% and diastolic blood pressure by 16% compared to people who do not practice gratitude. This shows without a doubt that practicing gratitude can physically enhance your performance. Make time to practice gratitude, and shave off a couple of seconds per mile on your next run.

Keep a gratitude journal along with your training log, and notice the correlation between your gratitude and your performance. Track your stats in your running and gratitude logs. Monitor how your physical performance has improved as you have written what you are grateful for every day.

Your gratitude journal will help you maintain positive energy, and your running will improve simply because your mind is in a positive space.

For a runner, joy comes from the run. It is how we relax after a day at the office. Constantly seeking to increase your pace, time, and distance, the challenge is to improve continuously. Imagine for a moment that you can make all of these improvements by simply being grateful.

Practice an Attitude of Gratitude

Decades of research have confirmed what we have inherently known: gratitude contributes to higher levels of happiness, positive emotional balance, and internal satisfaction.

According to clinical psychologist Dr. Justin Ross, running could be a mental health game-changer.

There are numerous ways you can incorporate gratitude into your life. As a runner consider doing a 'gratitude run.'

What is a gratitude run?

'Gratitude runs' have gained recognition as an effective tool for mental and physical health. For regular runners, gratitude runs are the same as normal runs. The only difference is your focus. Follow these steps until these special runs feel as natural as your other training.

1. **Lace up**. Stick to your usual pre-run habits. Wear what you feel comfortable in. Decide on a route, or let the road lead you.

2. **Set your mind**. You don't have to have a predetermined goal for this run. Simply think of the things in life you are grateful for—such as friends, family, and the ability to run, work, and enjoy life. Add special memories that have brought you happiness—things that you enjoy. Maybe ice cream? You get the gist. Let your mind flow. You will find that once you start, the thoughts keep coming.
3. **Consider each thought**. While you are running, reflect on what you are grateful for. Use this time away from normal training to resolve issues you might be experiencing. Is there negativity or self-doubt in your mind? Acknowledge the emotion, examine it, and search for how you can be grateful for what you have. For example, you might find yourself thinking about how grateful you are for your career. But this is followed by thoughts of stress related to your job. Acknowledge this trigger of anxiety. Allow yourself to feel the related emotions for a moment, and then let them fly into the light of your multitude of gratitude.
4. **Let it flow**. Many people find running a meditative exercise. Even if it is different for you, remember that this is not a training run. Coach your mind and emotions to feel the difference between a training run and a gratitude run, and then just let it flow. As you do more gratitude runs, you will find that the grateful thoughts resonate deep inside your inner

self. Let it flow because the more these thoughts resonate, the more you will feel the benefits until gratitude becomes a habit.

5. **Bottom line**? Gratitude is a practice that becomes a part of who we are. The more grateful we are, the more we will find things to be grateful for. By incorporating gratitude runs into your life, your enjoyment of them will increase as they become a part of your routine.

I found an amazing coach for myself. She is extremely knowledgeable about the sport and helped me progress toward achieving my goals in tremendous ways. But even more, she taught me one thing I never signed up for: gratitude. In my view, these are the best teachers because they teach beyond the obvious. Sometimes in life, we get more. She never told me to train with gratitude, but I can see that her heart, her soul, and every action she takes are filled with gratitude. It is part of her, and it is indeed infectious. We learn much more from observation and imitating what we observe than from intellectual understanding. Find yourself a coach, a role model, a group, or a running friend who teaches you something beyond the obvious.

"And above all, watch with glittering eyes the whole world around you because the greatest secrets are always hidden in the most unlikely places. Those who don't believe in magic will never find it." — Roald Dahl

Meditation

For Westerners, meditation has always seemed a practice from the east, but in the last four decades, there has been a total shift. People all over the world have seen how mediation improves the mind, body, and spirit.

My aunt started practicing meditation in the late 1990s and drove an hour to join guided meditation groups because there were none where she lived. Naturally, she told some friends and family members that she had started meditating. Wow! Their attitude blew her away. The questions about Eastern religions and philosophies came flying at her, but she told them that religion is not a part of meditation. Meditation is simply sitting in a relaxed pose or even reclining—whatever pose you feel most comfortable in —and focusing your mind on nothing.

It was difficult for her in the beginning as thoughts kept coming into her mind—odd thoughts, such as her grocery list and the fact that she needed to do a presentation at work. Eventually, she was taught by the 'yogi' or 'guru' to acknowledge her thoughts and let them go. After four weeks, she was very comfortable with meditating in a group at a guided meditation, but she decided to meditate at home in the early evening instead. She would light a solitary white candle, sit on her carpet, legs crossed, and focus on the flame. As the thoughts came, she acknowledged them and let them go.

She soon felt like a different person. After a stressful day at the office, her meditation became her personal time to give back to her mind, body, and spirit. She never spoke about her personal meditation as it was strangely unfamiliar to her circle of friends. These evening meditations helped her let go of the stress experienced throughout the day, calmed her down for the next day, and promoted restful sleep.

Sometime in her busy life, she stopped meditating. Looking back now, she can see the benefits she gained. She decided to start meditating again at this stage of her life and had everything ready—the carpet, the cushion, and the candle. However, she seemed to find excuses daily as to why she was not practicing meditation. So, she set a goal, which was to begin meditating again after the completion of this book. All the best to my aunt on her (flying) carpet!

Meditation Techniques

On the first steps of your journey to mindful meditation, you might feel overwhelmed. This can cause anxiety, but it is important to understand that you simply need to relax for a couple of minutes each day.

Once you have started on your journey into meditation, it can be an effective way to manage stress and anxiety. Meditation teaches you to take a breath and slow down. It calms your mind, body, and spirit.

Research has shown that gender, age, and geographic location do not matter when it comes to the effective use of meditation.

In 2015, nursing students who were taught mindful meditation techniques were less stressed and didn't suffer from anxiety. And a study of U.S. adolescents who suffered from anxiety benefited from learning meditation techniques.

How to Practice Meditation

When you start meditating, it can be challenging. Bear in mind that your mind has to train itself to become silent and aware of sitting still. Meditate for a few minutes at first, and once you are used to it, lengthen the sessions.

Establish a time and place that suits your needs. Find an area in your home where you won't be disturbed. Wear comfortable clothing, and sit or recline in a position that won't distract you. Close your eyes and breathe. Aim for regularly meditating at around the same time of day.

Become aware of yourself in the moment. While you are sitting comfortably, start to focus on your innermost thoughts and emotions. Inhale. Exhale. Breathe naturally; the rhythm of your breathing will adapt in time. If your thoughts wander, acknowledge them, and let them go. Focus on your breathing—inhale, then exhale.

Meditation is a personal practice. Find what resonates within you. When you are finished, open your eyes, and reflect on your thoughts and emotions.

Slowly get up, and do some gentle stretching.

Different Styles of Meditation

If you are at the beginning of your quest into meditation, guided meditation is where you should start. Once you know what meditation is about, you can look at the various styles of meditation and decide which one suits your lifestyle best.

The following are meditation techniques for beginners. Determine which of them resonates within you. Choose the techniques that make you most relaxed and tune you in to your innermost being.

Tapping

Tapping integrates the mind with the body by using acupressure and psychology. The practice of Ayurveda over thousands of years uses 'marma' points on the body to release toxins and promote cell regeneration. By applying pressure to these points, you can rid your body of negative emotions. First, identify a negative emotion such as fear or anger. Then, while holding that emotion in your mind, tap five, seven, or nine times on the meridian that corresponds with that emotion. Enthusiasts of tapping say that they feel their nervous system calm down.

Sound Meditation

Listening to music is meditation. Simply relax, and let the music tune into your soul. Allow the music to absorb you. Listen to an online sound bath or singing bowls, perhaps combined with sounds of nature. Alternatively, you can listen to your own selection of music.

Relaxing and soothing music without vocals creates harmony in your body. Harmonize with the music, and feel positive thoughts while listening to positive sounds.

Guided Meditation

There are many apps available that will take you through a guided meditation to get started. Yoga teachers suggest using an app with your favorite guided meditation. Listening to a guided meditation is good for a beginner and allows you to practice mindfulness.

Triangle Meditation

Triangle meditation is a good starting point for a beginner. Relax in a comfortable position. Close your eyes. Now take four counts of breath, and visualize up the side of the triangle to the top. Pause. Exhale four counts of breath, and visualize going down the other side of the triangle. Follow this with another four counts to complete the triangle. Continue this practice as long as it feels good.

Body Scanning

Lie in a comfortable position. Now close your eyes. Take a few moments to settle and relax. When you feel ready, focus on your toes and feet. Visualize any discomfort in that area. Breathe deeply, and feel the breath move into your feet. Allow your breath to blow away the pain. Then move up toward your legs, your arms, your spine, and all the way to the top of your head. Begin with 15 to 20 minutes a day of body scanning.

Loving-Kindness Meditation

Also known as a 'metta meditation,' loving-kindness meditation focuses your energy and thoughts on compassion and love. Write down a loving-kindness mantra that includes friends, family, and even the world. Sit in a comfortable position on a cushion, a rug, or even your bed. Now close your eyes and say the mantra out loud. Sharing your love and compassion with the world will bring about a change in you.

Walking Meditation

Mindfulness is meditation if you are present in the moment, taking a walk through nature, and becoming aware of your thoughts will activate your senses. Feel your feet touch the ground, hear the wind in the trees and the rustle of the leaves beneath your feet. Breathe in and relax. Now breathe in again and relax further. Turn your awareness to your breath. As you breathe in, feel the emotions that are coming to mind—anger, fear, judgment. Now as you breathe out, allow these emotions to flow out of your body. The movement of your feet in nature will keep your mind present and in a state of meditation and relaxation.

The possibilities are endless, and the idea is to have fun. Be curious, try things out, and establish your own rituals. For me, mindfulness brought many blessings into my life, especially when I feel tense or compete in races. Doing all the physical hard work in training requires stillness, and that might not naturally come when you are wired to do more and more. Our strength comes in knowing our weaknesses and nurturing those things as well. I make better decisions now and see patterns I didn't notice before.

How Runners Can Find a Coach

If you have decided that running is your game, you need to find a name!

Training plans, running apps, and websites are filled with tips from runners and coaches, but the trick is to find the best way to improve your running. Whether it's a coach or an app, it's personal, and you are unique!

Initially train yourself, but as you get better and the running gets easier and you know you love it, hire a personal coach.

Coaches might seem pricey, but long before the time you are training for your 51st marathon, you need an expert. Don't train for years in silence by yourself to discover running secrets that you could have applied in all of the previous 50 marathons. Coaches will tailor your training plan and choice of marathons and give you one-on-one guidance. Some coaches even include nutrition planning to help you reach prime condition to reach your goal.

If you are saying "I'm 55 and will never be a runner," stop! You *are* a runner!

Ask around the area where you run, perhaps at the local college or university, about coaches. There are many available options for all budgets. You might just join a running class or group for one session to get some expert tips and then go out on your own. Online coaching is also a viable option.

Bear in mind that not only must your coach be able to train you, but your personalities need to gel. You want to enjoy your training and look forward to learning something new. Most of all, you want to reach your goal. The right trainer and the right fit are key!

Be Inspired!

Eliud Kipchoge is arguably the greatest runner in history. He attributes his success to a simple lifestyle and his training routine. He uses no running apps and has no nutritional secrets to power him like a lightning rod when he runs and races.

According To Eliud, "I don't have extra money to actually make my mind go haywire. I am a human being, and I stay as a human being. Money stays away. I'm not working with money; money is in the bank. I want to live a simple life."

As a young boy in Kapsisiywa, Nandi County, Kenya, Eliud was unknowingly training for his future career when he ran to school and back each day. After school, he would get on his bicycle and do another 40K (almost a marathon distance!) to collect foodstuff and sell milk to the farmers in the area.

In 2002, Eliud qualified for the IAAF World Cross Country Championships as a Kenyan junior (under-20) representative. The Dublin event was an eye-opener for Eliud, and he realized that this was his passion. He won gold as part of the Kenyan Junior Team. In 2003, he won the gold again at the IAAF World Cross Country Senior Championships in Switzerland, setting a new record in the process.

This was only the beginning. Eliud's remarkable record includes gold medals attained at the 2016 and 2020 Olympic Games and the current marathon world record from the Berlin Marathon in 2022. His time was an amazing 2:01:09.

Eliud says his success comes from his heart and mind more than his legs, pace, and training. Eliud runs from the heart and soul!

Simplicity in All Things

In an interview with the BBC, Eliud said, “Our life here is simple, very simple. I get up in the morning, go for a run, come back. If it is a day for cleaning, we do the cleaning, or we just relax. Then go for lunch, massage, the four o’clock run, evening tea, relax, go to sleep. As simple as that.”

His training camp in Kenya is far from home, but he still goes home often, telling *Runner’s World* magazine, “Being away from the kids is really hard as they all want to see Daddy. I stay in training camp because of my memory of being motivated. We share ideas and show the young guys that it’s good to live together.”

Typically, a day at the training camp in Kaptagat, Eliud trains twice a day, six days a week, starting at 5:45 a.m. He runs between 124 and 135 miles per week. Twice a week, he focuses on strength and mobility, working on the muscle groups in his glutes, hamstrings, and core. For strength training, he likes to do planks, bridges, and single-leg deadlifts. The goal of the strength and mobility training is to create balance and avoid injuries.

Eliud has been keeping a training journal since 2003. It includes distances, times, exercises, massages, and the types of trainers he uses—especially how he feels when he wears specific trainers.

His nutrition is simple. He drinks three liters of water daily and eats a diet of home-baked bread, ugali (a dense maize-flour porridge), local fruits and vegetables, and meat.

Interestingly, he doesn't use supplements and believes that his body gets the right nutrients. He has enough energy and stamina, so he doesn't need to supplement.

Eliud believes in going to bed at 9 p.m. and waking at around 5 a.m. When he feels like a nap at any time during the day, he listens to his body and takes one.

According to Eliud, staying at the training camp promotes camaraderie and allows him to focus on his training.

Eliud is a prime example of prevailing based on natural talent, discipline, and hard work, not state-of-the-art equipment and dietitians and coaches. The simplicity of running is what brings Eliud into harmony with nature and allows him to draw strength, speed, and power from the natural elements that surround us.

Chapter 8
Building Your Inner Self

"Don't be afraid to fail. It's not the end of the world, and in many ways, it's the first step towards learning something better and getting better at it."

— Jon Hamm

Crush Your Self-Confidence

Don't just have self-confidence. *Crush it!*

Boost Your Bravery

Because it is the key to your success, runners need to follow strategies to build their self-confidence. Whether you just ran your 10th marathon or your very first 5K run, chances are good that you will have self-doubt.

Let's not kid ourselves here. When we have a bad run or when our training hasn't brought the satisfaction we expected, we feel a lack of self-confidence creeping into our subconscious minds.

Never fear—there are proven ways to gain self-confidence during periods when you are feeling that you haven't achieved your goals or have not nailed the time you set for your marathon.

Runners' Hurdles

Don't let negative feelings stop you from reaching your potential. What follows are the top six ways to reach the pinnacle of your running performance potential. They have been perfected and worked on to help you reach your goals. Aim to integrate these principal strategies into your mental preparation for training and racing.

- **Stop Self-Doubt**

Self-doubt is normal even among elite professional runners. Anxiety is a feeling most people experience at some point, whether you are being interviewed for a new job, doing a presentation, or standing at the starting line of a race. But there is 'healthy fear,' and there is 'destructive fear.' Healthy fear is beneficial as it puts all your cells into high gear and ready for the starting pistol. Healthy fear helps you stay motivated and ready to face any challenge. Destructive fear just makes you scared.

- **Perfect Preparation**

Remember that you can only prepare for the elements that pertain to *your* race. Elements like the weather and other unknowns are beyond your control, so focus on what you *can* control. Think about which gear you'll wear in the race, familiarize yourself with timed eating for fuel, and make a hydration plan that works for you. Find and fine-tune a runner's checklist as you pack your bags and set out your apparel for race day. Then go through the list to ensure that you have everything you need. Having complete control over the little things allows you to focus on the big things.

- **Sensible Self-Talk**

If you are feeling negative, you are probably allowing ANTs (Automatic Negative Thoughts syndrome) to lead you to negative self-talk. Stop for a moment to give yourself a pep talk. One of the best ways to counteract ANTs is to develop a positive running mantra. Use this mantra whenever you feel self-doubt creeping into your thoughts. Try these: "I feel ready for this race." "I am fit and can run this marathon." "I am strong and well-prepared for this race."

Research has shown that your subconscious mind influences your conscious mind, and soon your thoughts can turn to action. Let positive feelings become a part of your daily life, not only in your running but in other areas as well.

- **Envision Yourself as an Elite Runner**

Visualize a runner who you admire. Now imagine yourself running with the same great form and at the same pace. Imagine you have been trained by that runner's coaches, and focus on attaining your goal. Pace yourself with your icon in mind, and you will be able to reach for the stars.

- **Remarkable Runs**

Yes, you have had remarkable runs—runs where everything has felt smooth and easy, effortless runs that you have enjoyed from start to finish. Stop your mind racing with negativity and visualize one of your most remarkable and enjoyable runs. Perfection in motion is your goal, and you can relax because you have trained for this.

- **Run with Self-Assured Runners**

If you are a newbie runner, find a group of runners who are at ease with themselves—runners who are optimistic, self-assured, and enjoy the bliss of running. These are the runners who will lift you up when you are having a bad day. These are the people who look at running as a positive exercise that can be enjoyed by everyone. If you join a group of runners with one or more pessimists who constantly make negative comments or complain while running, find another group. Unfortunately, negativity is contagious, and it is something you don't want to catch. Take your trainers and lace them up with a group that exudes joyful optimism.

Fear of Failure

What is fear of failure?

Fear of failure is formally called atychiphobia. It's a difficult name for a difficult emotion that might never cross your path. The fact is that it's a stealthy emotion of which we may not always be aware. The fear of failure is for some people so debilitating that they don't go anywhere or try new activities because they are fearful of failing. The flip side of the coin is that they are missing out on so many wonderful things in life. Simply put, they are so afraid of failure that they aren't able to live their best lives.

While it's true that people do fail at certain things they try, failure mostly means growth and learning to overcome challenges. Overcoming a challenge gives you the experience to be ready for any other challenges that come your way. Failure is not an example of inadequacy. It is merely part of a learning curve that will lead you to achieve greater things in life. It is learning by practice; many successful people have overcome failure and ended up at the top of their field.

Michael Jordan: This superstar is considered by many to be the greatest basketball player of all time. If you examine his history, you can hardly believe that he was cut from his high school basketball team because his coach said he lacked skill.

Babe Ruth: This baseball legend of a century ago had a lifetime batting average of .342. Translated into a percentage, that means that 65% of the time he batted, he did *not* get a hit. This makes him sound like a failure as he 'failed' almost two-thirds of the time at the plate, though, in fact, his career batting average still ranks 10th in history. (Hitting a hard-thrown ball is hard!) What's most important is that Babe Ruth loved the game and loved life, and even though at times he experienced batting slumps as every player does, he enjoyed the journey as much as the destination.

Warren Buffett: This brilliant businessman and investor was rejected by Harvard University Business School.

Richard Branson: Owner of the Virgin Group and world-famous entrepreneur doesn't even have a high school diploma. But he decided to pursue the impossible, and he did!

Accept failure as a part of life, and learn from your insights. Failure should be regarded as something to learn from and be motivated by as you face future challenges.

Now put on your trainers and give it a go!

Symptoms of Fear of Failure

In order to change your mindset from being held captive by a fear of failure, you must first recognize where your fears originate.

According to Dr. Albert Ellis, a psychologist, behavioral therapist, and founder of REBT (Rational Emotive Behavioral Psychology), your aim should be to confront your fears. Uncover your irrational beliefs that are creating these fears and sabotaging your life, then confront your beliefs and replace them with rational thoughts.

These are signs that make you feel threatened and result in an irrational fear of failure:

- Becoming impatient if your performance at a race is less than perfect
- Focusing on the outcome of a race instead of living in the moment
- Feeling unvalued by your competitors or family
- Making assumptions about other people's thoughts of your performance
- Going into fight, flight, or freeze mode before a race

Reluctance to Accept Challenges

When you are reluctant to take on a new challenge, whether in sports, at work, or at home, it is a way of protecting yourself because you fear you might fail at a new activity. For a runner, that might translate into running a half-marathon instead of a full marathon.

Self-Sabotage

Procrastination, anxiety, and the failure to attain your goals due to myriad excuses are all forms of self-sabotage. Self-sabotage is directly related to a fear of failure.

Low Self-Confidence

Self-esteem and self-confidence

Low self-esteem or self-confidence can be seen when a person constantly uses negative terms when talking about themselves or their achievements. Negative statements such as "I'm not talented enough to get that promotion" or "I'm going to keep up with my fast friend at the next marathon" are examples of low self-confidence. Replace these negative words with positive words such as, "I'm going to upskill myself and request a promotion this year" or "I'm going to train hard and join my friend for this upcoming marathon." Remember, your subconscious is listening.

Chasing Perfection

Constantly striving for perfection is not healthy. You need to find a balance between perfectionism and reality. In reality, if you don't have perfect eye-hand coordination, it is not logical to try out for baseball, but you may have a talent for speed, so try running. Do what your body is meant to do, and enjoy the things that you are good at. Chances are you will be successful.

Common Sources of Fear in Athletes

Athletes are under a lot of pressure to perform, but this at times leads to a fear of failure, which in turn affects performance. Personal fear of failure when you are part of a team creates extra anxiety and stress. (Running is not necessarily a team sport, but many runners find themselves joining running clubs and teams that compete locally, regionally, nationally, or internationally.) These emotions are felt by the entire team and, in turn, may affect the performance of the team overall. As part of a team, athletes tend to assume they are perceived in a certain manner, and their success or failure has negative consequences on the team's performance. They are concerned about letting their coach or team down or disappointing their friends and family. These concerns are often unfounded, but it is important to understand that to the athlete, it is of extreme importance, which leads to anxiety and stress. Athletes often seek social approval, and they assume they will get recognition and approval only when they win.

These fears, although internalized, negatively affect the athlete. Here are some examples:

- **Fear of negative social evaluation**: This causes you to feel that other people only value you when you win in your chosen sport.
- **Fear of losing a match or a race**: When you have trained hard and expect to win but think you might not, you live in a state of fear of failure.
- **Fear of embarrassment**: This is when the athlete is afraid to be embarrassed in front of their peers or family.
- **Fear of not performing well**: Feeling the need to meet the expectations of others increases mental and physical pressure on the athlete and can paradoxically produce a poor performance.
- **Fear of letting others down**: Most people have family and friends who have high expectations of athletes. Unintentionally, this places immense pressure on the athlete as they don't want to let anyone down.

Overcoming Fear of Failure

Life is filled with obstacles, whether in one's social, personal, career, or sports pursuits. The bottom line is this: Are you going to let fear prevent you from leading your life, or are you going to see obstacles as part of a learning curve that will help you achieve your goals? We should embrace the challenges we face and sometimes, to put it simply, just 'go with the flow.' Life is exciting, so live it to the fullest extent. Don't let fear hold you back!

Positivity: Is the glass half-full or half-empty? Guess what? It doesn't matter. If the glass is half-full, add more liquid. (It's never half-empty, by the way!) It's as easy as that. Positive thinking is critical if you want to succeed. Positivity gives you power over your thoughts and keeps you going through the tough times.

What is the worst-case scenario? Honestly, what can be that bad? Okay, so you didn't win a trophy, but you got to spend quality time with friends, and you may have traveled to different places. Runners, it's okay. You didn't win, but remember all those joyful training sessions when it was just you and your run.

Different Outcomes: If you are really feeling anxious, think of other potential outcomes. This might make you less fearful. People fear the unknown, but if you make a list of what you fear or what the less desirable outcomes are, you might realize that you are well-equipped to deal with anything that comes your way.

In a Nutshell...

If you live with a fear of failure, you will be trapped in emotions like anxiety and fear, just like an insect in a spider's web with more and more threads trapping you in your fear.

Overcoming this fear takes a purposeful effort to change your perspectives and beliefs. It is called 'reframing' to look at the same situation from a different angle. See the situation from a more realistic angle instead of letting your emotions cloud your view, and your fear will dissipate.

Write down how rational or irrational the source of your fear really is. This means evaluating how failing or succeeding will affect your life as a whole. Make a list of positive and negative facts, and be realistic about each one.

You will discover how rational or irrational the source of your fear is. For example, do you know for a fact that your peers, friends, family, and coach will lose respect for you if you miss your targeted marathon time?

Write down what you do know is a fact. You are loved by all these people for many reasons, and this love supersedes the little things in life.

Finally...

Fear of Missing Out

FOMO may be the buzzword (well, buzz acronym) of the century. But it is one of many 21st-century buzzwords. Everything we say today must be said faster, and everything we do must be done quicker than the speed of light. These acronyms keep me scrambling to keep up, and even that is sometimes quite a mission.

FOMO is the acronym for Fear of Missing Out.

Athletes succumb to FOMO because they harbor thoughts or perceptions that others are having more fun, living better lives, or enjoying better experiences. These thoughts lead to negative emotions, especially envy.

The FOMO phenomenon is becoming a worldwide trend, mostly due to photos and video clips on social media and, because most people have instant access to smartphones, laptops, and iPads, there is no escaping the constant stream of beautiful people doing amazing things. This phenomenon adds to the basic stressors of life and, in some people, evokes a sense of not fitting in with peers. This, in turn, leads to psychological trauma.

FOMO, the idea of missing out on something, can be traced back to research by Dan Herman, a marketing strategist who coined the phrase in 1996 after watching advertisements of good-looking young people using a specific product. The response from people seeing others looking good and purchasing and enjoying the product had an almost automatic effect. They assumed that if they also used that product, they would also be part of the 'in' crowd.

Social media has made FOMO a more common phenomenon as people only post pictures of themselves having a great time—the picture-perfect highlights of their lives. Seeing these fabulous photos on social media has created an unrealistic view of reality, as social media users' sense of 'normal' has been negatively affected. Social media has resulted in the perception that 'my life is better than your life' and tends to make people look at their lives from a negative perspective when compared to the social media posts of others.

In reality, we all feel as if we are missing out on some things that others are enjoying. To combat this emotion, focus and reflect on all the good things in your life—your family, your friends, and all the other people and things in your life you are grateful for.

Stop!

Stop focusing on what everyone else is doing, and enjoy the best parts of your life. Overcome your challenges, and grow and learn. Trust me, real life is much more exciting than living an artificial life through social media.

Curb Your Cravings

Stop your craving for checking your social media accounts by implementing these top tips:

- **Ditch Digital**

Schedule a weekend where you don't check your social media and simply live in the moment—*your* moment. Do things you never have time for. Paint your room, spend time with your pets, lie on the grass, or read a book. Learn to enjoy the simple things in life. You might find they bring you unbelievable pleasure.

- **Fabulous Focus**

Focus on the small things in life. Enjoy your surroundings, and listen to your favorite music. My favorite quote by Nietzsche is: “And those who were seen dancing were thought to be insane by those who could not hear the music.” To me, that means to dance like no one is watching. Live your life to the fullest no matter what others might think or say!

- **Find a Friend**

Connect with fellow human beings in person, whether at the park or the shopping mall. Smile at a stranger, and say hello. Social media isn’t real, so be real. Reality is fun. Go to a social engagement that you would normally avoid. Smile, listen to music, and enjoy yourself. You might have the time of your life. Remember the ugly duckling that turned into a beautiful swan? Your swan is just waiting for you to set it free.

Be Inspired! Olympian Allyson Felix effects Changes

For a female track athlete, pregnancy is referred to as the ‘kiss of death.’ This was the case for Allyson Felix. As an Olympic champion and entrepreneur, this did not seem right for a variety of reasons, so she set out to change the policy of sponsors and the Olympic Board of Directors. She wanted this attitudinal change to be a global phenomenon.

Allyson is the most decorated Olympian in track and field in the current century. No other woman has won as many gold medals (seven) in Olympic history, and she has been a preeminent force in the running world for many years.

When Allyson found out she was pregnant, she was elated, only to be confronted by her sponsor's maternity policy. In 2018, she had to have an emergency C-section when her daughter Camryn was born. Her sponsor at the time gave her what she described as "unfair compensation" for a postpartum athlete. She decided it was time to change the worldview on pregnancy in female athletes.

Allyson said she wanted the world to be different for her daughter and other female athletes following in her footsteps. She immediately took action, using her experience as a disciplined athlete to follow a new path—promoting and effecting policy changes in the world of sports. She started a family while advocating for the policy change in her former sponsor's policy.

This was an accomplishment that went above and beyond all expectations as she ensured these policy changes would pave the way for future female athletes.

Allyson's actions and ultimate win proved that if you believe in yourself and your cause, you can advocate for major changes that will be beneficial for the future of all.

"You don't have to be an Olympian to create change for yourself and others," she says. "Each of us can bet on ourselves."

Allyson is not only an Olympian. We can't wait to see what comes next as she announced in 2022 that she was stepping away from running but would be active in other areas of importance.

Chapter 9
Happily Ever After

“Jack, I was so happy to see you cheering me on near the finish! When I reached the marathon finish line, I was so relieved. My stomach gave me problems after I passed 21 miles, but once I saw you, I knew everything would be okay.” Jeanne then admired the beautiful view from atop the mountain that they had first ‘conquered’ on their fateful first run almost a year before.

As they sat on the picnic blanket, Jack planted a kiss on her forehead and said, “Who knew that a run could have so many benefits? Being in nature brought me such harmony, and I met the woman of my dreams! I have learned so much from you, Jeanne.” Jack opened their picnic backpack as they had taken a leisurely hike to the pinnacle of the mountain. “Look, I packed the perfect runner’s foods. For starters, we have whole-wheat crackers and hummus, the perfect mix of carbs and proteins from the chickpeas, followed by a turkey sandwich on whole-wheat bread, and for dessert, strawberries dipped in dark chocolate."

"I am so impressed with your menu, Jack, which means you have been listening to my nutrition planning. And I thought you were simply agreeing with everything I said to not start a food argument." Jeanne laughed.

"There is only one thing that is not allowed on the runner's menu, but today is a special occasion," said Jack.

"Come on, Jack, out with it. The suspense is too much," Jeanne teased.

Jack reached into the picnic backpack and pulled out a bottle of Dom Perignon champagne. Jeanne then gasped as he reached for something in his pocket and pulled out a small square box.

Jack crouched on bended knee and opened the blue velvet box. Inside was the most gorgeous diamond ring Jeanne had ever seen.

"Jeanne, my love, would you do me the honor of becoming my wife?" asked Jack, almost holding his breath for her answer.

"Yes, yes, a million times yes! You have been my inspiration this past year, helping me follow a nutritious diet, taking me to the gym for strength training, spending my rest days with me... Oh Jack, yes, yes, yes!" an elated Jeanne almost squealed.

Jack slipped the perfectly-sized ring onto Jeanne's finger and kissed her. She felt as if they were in heaven. It was the perfect place and the perfect time.

Then Jack drew back slightly. "There is more," he said. "After I gave you that book about marathon running, nutrition, and mindset, I have been watching you and seen that your training has made you stronger and faster as a runner but also stronger in your resolve to live holistically. This has led me to the decision that I am going to sign up for a marathon too. From now on, I am going to run with you, train with you, practice gratitude with you, and change my mindset as you have during the past year."

"Oh Jack, I couldn't be happier than I am right now, except perhaps when we do our first marathon together and cross the finish line," said Jeanne.

Jack popped the cork and poured them each a glass. They looked at each other and the mountain and valley and knew that from that day forward, they would be a team—in running *and* in their personal lives!

Afterword

Running is very personal and unique to each runner. I believe in the science of running and the art of running. The science is covered in all of the chapters you just read, and of course, there is plenty more knowledge available. Naturally, some information is conflicting, but the most important part is you. Without you, there is no running, and this is where the art begins.

It is you who gives your running purpose, joy, and meaning. It is a learning process that will last as long as you allow it, no matter your age, experience, or goals. You're the boss, remember?

Your task is to make it work for you. I can tell you what worked for me and suggest techniques and tools, but I cannot make you run or change your mindset. That power is within you. The more I learned about running, ironically, the more questions I had. But it is the questions, far more than the answers, that keep us on our toes and keep us excited and alive. Learning never stops, and I hope you had some questions answered in this book, but even more, I hope you now have some new questions.

Running is so much more than putting one foot in front of the other; it is about who you become and about new possibilities. Through running, you might meet the love of your life, come up with a business idea, or make new friends. The possibilities are limitless. Start dreaming!

While preparing for a job interview, did you ever think about your strengths and weaknesses—and then came up with examples during the interview and felt good about them? Then a couple of months later, someone asked you about your strengths and weaknesses, but you blanked out. You forgot them, just like that! While running, you will experience your strengths and weaknesses because they will be visible, and once you learn to master them, you will 'play wild cards' in all areas of your life.

The Most Important Ingredient is Action

Many people, some even more talented or skilled than me, don't take action, or their actions are so small and inconsistent that a light breeze will shake them and swallow not only their goal but also their dream. That is not you! You are a serious runner; you are committed to your goal. This is your joy!

Ready, Set, Go!

Take action now. Sign up for a race, go for a run, shop for a running outfit, but *do something—anything!*

Acknowledgments

Even though crossing the finish line seems often a solo act, it is usually the result of a team effort. I would like to share some special thank you note.

To my parents - my biggest fans - traveling the world and at times letting their fear whisper: “Again? Is this not too much? Okay, you know best!”

My sister for cheering me on and greeting me at the finish line with a smile while waiting for hours because my stomach had different plans.

My friends for supporting me emotionally and mentally, occasionally also reminding me: “You will need to sell a lot of books.” Yes, I know (with a smile)!

One enthusiastic friend, who completed several half marathons before the official race day while never considering any hydration plan – you definitely need this book!

My core running team as in my running coach, Yvonne, for teaching me so much more than running. My physiotherapist, Joe, for keeping my body oiled and happy and for Eden, my massage angel, – a massage comes always handy.

A special thank you also to Nita, Jeanne and Robert for giving this book a form and voice.

And of course, to you for reading my book!

Thank you.

About the Author

Heinke Kauntz is a certified personal trainer, a sports fanatic, a curious lifetime student and a passionate believer in self-development. After serving her sentence as a corporate slave with 7+ years of marketing experience she decided it was time to move on and from now on only work on her dreams.

Starting with her first book: *You're the Boss: Make Running Work for you,* Heinke wanted to share her joy, journey and wisdom with you. As a triathlete, running was always her favorite discipline – "*it just felt right!*"

Through her challenges and the mental, emotional and spiritual training, she realized that running was indeed the perfect tool to not only make her a *better runner*, but ultimately a *better person*, and it gave her the necessary grit to *hang in* on all her dreams.

Follow on Instagram at: you_retheboss

References

10k Training Plan for Beginners. (n.d.). Retrieved 2023, from Runner's World Shop: https://store.runnersworld.com/beginners-10k-plan.html

25 OF THE TOP SHOES RIGHT NOW! (n.d.). Retrieved 2023, from Runners World: https://www.runnersworld.com/

Ackerman, C. E. (2018, July 5). *Positive Mindset: How to Develop a Positive Mental Attitude*. Retrieved from Positive Psychology: https://positivepsychology.com/positive-mindset/

Ambassador Spotlight: Meb Keflezighi. (n.d.). Retrieved 2023, from Live Aloha: https://livealoha.mauijim.com/live/aloha/

Baker, C. (2022, May 19). *Change Your Life With Atomic Habits*. Retrieved from Leaders: https://leaders.com/articles/personal-growth/atomic-habits/

Barker, E. (2016, June 7). *This Is The Best Way to Overcome Fear of Missing Out*. Retrieved from TIME: https://time.com/4358140/overcome-fomo/

Bieler, K. (2006, August 30). *What To Drink When*. Retrieved from Runner's World: https://www.runnersworld.com/nutrition-weight-loss/a20803500/a-hydration-guide-for-runners/

Brandt, A. P. (2018, July 30). *Science Proves That Gratitude Is Key to Well-Being*. Retrieved from Psychology Today: https://www.psychologytoday.com/us/blog/mindful-anger/201807/science-proves-gratitude-is-key-well-being

Brooks, A. C. (2021, February 25). *Go Ahead and Fail.* Retrieved from The Atlantic: https://www.theatlantic.com/family/archive/2021/02/how-overcome-fear-failure/618130/

Brown, J., & Wong, J. (2017, June 6). *How Gratitude Changes You and Your Brain.* Retrieved from Greater Good Magazine: https://greatergood.berkeley.edu/article/item/how_gratitude_changes_you_and_your_brain

Canning, K., & Del Turco, L. (2021, April 14). *Your Fitness Plateau And Sleep Problems Might Actually Be Signs Of Overtraining.* Retrieved from Women's Health: https://www.womenshealthmag.com/fitness/a27562920/signs-of-overtraining-recovery/

Capano, C. (2020, June 16). *Five Keys To Maintaining A Positive Mindset.* Retrieved from Forbes: https://www.forbes.com/sites/forbescoachescouncil/2020/06/16/five-keys-to-maintaining-a-positive-mindset/?sh=376a43147da9

Caple, J. (2016, August 14). *Usain Bolt is an inspiration to millions, so who's next?* Retrieved from ESPN: https://www.espn.com/olympics/trackandfield/story/_/id/17306198/olympics-2016-usain-bolt-inspiration-millions-next

Cherry, K. (2022, September 2). *Benefits of Mindfulness.* Retrieved from Very Well Mind: https://www.verywellmind.com/the-benefits-of-mindfulness-5205137

Cherry, K. (2022, September 20). *What Is a Mindset and Why It Matters.* Retrieved from Very Well Mind: https://www.verywellmind.com/what-is-a-mindset-2795025

Cherry, K. (2022, September 8). *What Is Meditation?* Retrieved from Very Well Mind: https://www.verywellmind.com/what-is-meditation-2795927

Cherry, K. (2023, February 22). *What Is Empathy?* Retrieved from Very Well Mind: https://www.verywellmind.com/what-is-empathy-2795562

Chertoff, J. (2018, April 17). *What Are the Benefits and Risks of Running Every Day?* Retrieved from Healthline: https://www.healthline.com/health/fitness-exercise/running-everyday

Clear, J. (n.d.). *Goal Setting: A Scientific Guide to Setting and Achieving Goals*. Retrieved 2023, from James Clear: https://jamesclear.com/goal-setting

Coach Jeff. (n.d.). *The Best Supplements for Runners*. Retrieved 2023, from Runners Connect: https://runnersconnect.net/the-best-supplements-for-runners/

Coach Jeff. (n.d.). *What to Eat Before a Run*. Retrieved 2023, from Runners Connect: https://runnersconnect.net/what-to-eat-before-a-run/

Collins, J. (n.d.). *Meal plans for runners*. Retrieved 2023, from Good Food: https://www.bbcgoodfood.com/howto/guide/running-nutrition-typical-training-plan

Connecting the World to Wellness. (n.d.). Retrieved 2023, from Mind Body: https://www.mindbodyonline.com/

Corrêa-Oliveira, R., Fachi, J. L., Vieira, A., Sato, F. T., & Vinolo, M. A. (2016, April). *Regulation of immune cell function by short-chain fatty acids*. Retrieved from PubMed: https://pubmed.ncbi.nlm.nih.gov/27195116/

Cuncic, A. (2023, January 24). *How to Handle Performance Anxiety as an Athlete*. Retrieved from Very Well Mind: https://www.verywellmind.com/how-do-i-handle-performance-anxiety-as-an-athlete-3024337

Damen, L. (n.d.). *7 Reasons Why Rest And Recovery Are Important To*

Runners. Retrieved 2023, from realbuzz.com: https://www.realbuzz.com/articles-interests/running/article/7-reasons-why-rest-and-recovery-are-important/

Darkins, R. (2017, February 5). *RUNNING FREE: WHAT USAIN BOLT TEACHES US ABOUT POSITIVE PSYCHOLOGY*. Retrieved from https://rorydarkins.com/blog-1/2017/2/5/running-free-what-usain-bolt-teaches-us-about-positive-psychology: https://rorydarkins.com/blog-1/2017/2/5/running-free-what-usain-bolt-teaches-us-about-positive-psychology

Davidson, K. M. (2021, September 21). *What's the Best Diet for Runners? Nutrition Tips and More*. Retrieved from Healthline: https://www.healthline.com/nutrition/runners-diet

Del Mistro, M. (2021, November 10). *Improve Your Running with Goal Setting*. Retrieved from Runstreet: https://www.runstreet.com/blog/goal-setting

Designed for Runners, by Runners: The Only Running Gear You Need! (n.d.). Retrieved 2023, from Fitletic.com: https://www.fitletic.com/

Douglas, S., & Brick, N. (2021, July 2). *How to Build Confidence as a Runner*. Retrieved from Runner's World: https://www.runnersworld.com/training/a36729025/how-to-build-confidence-as-a-runner/

Douglas, S., & Keflezighi, M. (2016, October 4). *Meb Keflezighi's 5 Drills to Make You a Better Runner*. Retrieved from Runner's World: https://www.runnersworld.com/training/a20824733/meb-keflezighis-5-drills-to-make-you-a-better-runner/

Edberg, H. (2022, May 11). *The Power of Gratitude: 5 Small Tips for a Happier Life*. Retrieved from The Positivity Blog: https://www.positivityblog.com/gratitude-tips/

Eidel, S. (n.d.). *Runner's Diet*. Retrieved 2023, from Johns Hopkins Medicine: https://www.hopkinsmedicine.org/health/wellness-and-prevention/runners-diet

Everheart, D. (2020, October 6). *Learn the Top 10 Tips for Mind and Body Wellness for Better Life Now*. Retrieved from The Art of Living: https://www.artofliving.org/us-en/meditation/meditation-for-you/mind-body-wellness

Fetters, A. K. (2021, July 6). *Post-Workout Muscle Recovery: How to Let Your Muscles Heal and Why*. Retrieved from Everyday Health: https://www.everydayhealth.com/fitness/post-workout-muscle-recovery-how-why-let-your-muscles-heal/

Feyoh, M. (2022, June 1). *57 Wellness Quotes to Build a Healthy Mindset (and Body)*. Retrieved from Develop Good Habits: https://www.developgoodhabits.com/wellness-quotes/

Fitzgerald, J. (2017, January 20). *How To Set Ambitious (But Realistic) Running Goals*. Retrieved from Strength Running: https://strengthrunning.com/2017/01/ambitious-goal-setting-for-runners/

Fleet Feet Editors. (2022). *How to Start Running: A Beginners Guide*. Retrieved from Fleet Feet: https://www.fleetfeet.com/how-to-start-running

Frey, M. M.-C. (2022, September 22). *How Long Should You Work Out*. Retrieved from Very Well Fit: https://www.verywellfit.com/how-long-should-i-work-out-3495483

Friedlander, J. (2018, December 4). *Tony Robbins' Secrets for Effective Goal Setting*. Retrieved from Success: https://www.success.com/tony-robbins-goals/

Frye, A. (2021). *How Being Coachable Made Usain Bolt An Olympic*

Legend. Retrieved from Forbes: https://www.forbes.com/sites/andyfrye/2021/07/21/how-being-coachable-made-usain-bolt-an-olympian-legend/?sh=33ab732d4a8c

Gelles, D. (n.d.). *How to Meditate*. Retrieved 2023, from The New York Times: https://www.nytimes.com/guides/well/how-to-meditate

Globokar, L. (2020, March 5). *The Power Of Visualization And How To Use It*. Retrieved from Forbes: https://www.forbes.com/sites/lidijaglobokar/2020/03/05/the-power-of-visualization-and-how-to-use-it/?sh=2af637966497

Goldberg, L. (n.d.). *The Secret to Happiness: 5 Tips to Feel More Grateful and Blissful*. Retrieved 2023, from Tiny Buddha: https://tinybuddha.com/blog/secret-happiness-5-tips-feel-grateful-blissful/

Gootman, J., & Kirousis, W. (2003, March 31). *Effective Goal Setting*. Retrieved from Runner's World: https://www.runnersworld.com/advanced/a20819775/effective-goal-setting/

Grez, M. (2021, March 15). *What Usain Bolt did next: Olympic legend on his greatest achievement and life after athletics*. Retrieved from CNN: https://www.cnn.com/2021/03/15/sport/usain-bolt-athletics-olympics-tokyo-2020-cmd-spt-intl/index.html

Guy-Evans, O. (2023, February 8). *How To Deal With FOMO In Your Life*. Retrieved from Simply Psychology: https://simplypsychology.org/how-to-cope-with-fomo.html

Hamlett, A. (2014, June 13). *RW's complete guide to running and hydration*. Retrieved from Runner's World: https://www.runnersworld.com/uk/nutrition/a761780/rws-complete-guide-to-hydration/

Health Coach & Hypnotherapist. (n.d.). Retrieved 2023, from Mind Body Wellness: https://www.mind-bodywellness.com/

Heins, W. (2021, December 22). *A New Approach to Goal-Setting for Runners in 2022.* Retrieved from The Mother Runners: https://www.themotherrunners.com/goal-setting-for-runners-in-2022/

Hendriksen, E. P. (2016, August 25). *How to Overcome FOMO.* Retrieved from Psychology Today: https://www.psychologytoday.com/us/blog/how-be-yourself/201608/how-overcome-fomo

Hendriksen, E. P. (2019, October 3). *5 Ways to Overcome Your Fear of Failure.* Retrieved from Psychology Today: https://www.psychologytoday.com/us/blog/how-to-be-yourself/201910/5-ways-to-overcome-your-fear-of-failure

Hinchman, W. (2020, January 31). *The 7 Best Supplements For Endurance Runners.* Retrieved from SWOLVERINE: https://swolverine.com/blogs/blog/supplements-for-endurance-runners

Ho, L. (2023, February 14). *10 Ways to Unlock Your Mind Power to Be More Successful.* Retrieved from Life Hack: https://www.lifehack.org/861733/mind-power

Hoge, A. (2022, April 24). *How To BELIEVE IN YOURSELF | Tony Robbins.* Retrieved from YouTube: https://www.youtube.com/watch?v=hU1uN_yO7aE

holistic adjective. (n.d.). Retrieved 2023, from Merriam-Webster: https://www.merriam-webster.com/dictionary/holistic

Holistic Running. (n.d.). Retrieved 2023, from wholisticrunning.com: https://wholisticrunning.com/holistic-running/

Hondorp, G. (2019, October 6). *The 'Gratitude Mile' Might Be the Trick*

You Need to Power Through Your Long Runs. Retrieved from Runner's World: https://www.runnersworld.com/training/a29321193/gratitude-tips-for-long-run/

Houston, E. B. (2019, April 9). *What is Goal Setting and How to Do it Well*. Retrieved from Positive Psychology: https://positivepsychology.com/goal-setting/

How to Believe in Yourself (Tony Robbins). (n.d.). Retrieved 2023, from Mind Stroll: https://introspectwriter.wordpress.com/2022/01/17/how-to-believe-in-yourself-tony-robbins/

Indeed Editorial Team. (2023, February 27). *10 Effective Goal-Setting Techniques for Achieving Your Goals*. Retrieved from indeed: https://www.indeed.com/career-advice/career-development/goal-setting-techniques

Jamshaid, F. D. (2021, February 15). *Goals vs. Systems — Atomic Habits*. Retrieved from Medium: https://medium.com/life-lemons/goals-vs-systems-atomic-habits-176a35bb36c8

Klein, G. P. (2016, May 1). *Mindsets*. Retrieved from Psychology Today: https://www.psychologytoday.com/us/blog/seeing-what-others-dont/201605/mindsets

Kline, K. (2015, December 26). *Why Rest Days are Important for Higher Efficiency at Work*. Retrieved from LifeHack: https://www.lifehack.org/347808/why-rest-days-are-important-for-higher-efficiency-work

Kumari, P. (2019, August 21). *The Inspirational Story Of Usain Bolt, Will Teach You To Never Stop Running For Your Dreams*. Retrieved from Scoop Whoop: https://www.scoopwhoop.com/sports/worlds-fastest-man-usian-bolt-life-story/

Lebow, H. I. (2021, July 12). *How Mindfulness and Gratitude Go Hand in*

Hand. Retrieved from Psych Central: https://psychcentral.com/blog/how-gratitude-and-mindfulness-go-hand-in-hand

Lechner, T. (2015, October 19). *How to Develop a Gratitude Mindset*. Retrieved from Chopra: https://chopra.com/articles/how-to-develop-a-gratitude-mindset

Lechner, T. (2019, November 26). *The Neuroscience Behind Gratitude: How Does Cultivating Appreciation Affect Your Brain?* Retrieved from Chopra: https://chopra.com/articles/the-neuroscience-behind-gratitude-how-does-cultivating-appreciation-affect-your-brain

Leicht, L. (2022, November 19). *What To Eat Before, During, and After Running*. Retrieved from health.com: https://www.health.com/fitness/what-to-eat-before-running

Lindstrom, S. (2022, August 17). *Usain Bolt Jamaican athlete*. Retrieved from Britannica: https://www.britannica.com/biography/Usain-Bolt

Luff, C. A.-C. (2022, January 3). *5K Training Plan for Beginners*. Retrieved from Very Well Fit: https://www.verywellfit.com/six-week-5k-training-schedule-2910850

Luff, C. A.-C. (2022, August 10). *8 Tips for Proper Running Form*. Retrieved from Very Well Fit: https://www.verywellfit.com/tips-for-proper-running-form-4020227

Luff, C. A.-C. (2022, August 10). *How to Start Running The Absolute Beginner's Guide to Running for Fun and Exercise*. Retrieved from Very Well Fit: https://www.verywellfit.com/how-to-start-running-the-absolute-beginners-guide-2911191

Marisa Peer. (2021, October 8). Retrieved from Wikita: https://wikitia.com/wiki/Marisa_Peer

Marks, H. (2022, April 15). *What Is Holistic Medicine?* Retrieved from Web MD: https://www.webmd.com/balance/what-is-holistic-medicine

Mateo, A. (2021, July 30). *4 Simple Steps To Optimize Post-Run Recovery.* Retrieved from Runner's World: https://www.runnersworld.com/health-injuries/a37095359/adjustments-to-optimize-recovery/

Mateo, A. (2021, October 19). *Exactly What to Do On Your Rest Days.* Retrieved from Runner's World: https://www.runnersworld.com/training/a37964113/what-to-do-on-rest-days/

Mayo Clinic Staff. (2022, October 11). *Mindfulness exercises.* Retrieved from Mayo Clinic: https://www.mayoclinic.org/healthy-lifestyle/consumer-health/in-depth/mindfulness-exercises/art-20046356

McCoy, P. (2021). *How To Start Out The New Year Right* . Retrieved from Rainmakers: https://gorainmakers.com/2020/12/14/goal-intentions-and-starting-out-2021-right/

Meditation and Mindfulness: What You Need To Know. (2022, June). Retrieved from National Center for Complementary and Integrative Health: https://www.nccih.nih.gov/health/meditation-and-mindfulness-what-you-need-to-know

Metzler, B. (2009, February 19). *Run Softly, Naturally* . Retrieved from Runner's World: https://www.runnersworld.com/advanced/a20846011/run-softly-naturally/

Miller, J. (2016, July 8). *8 Ways To Have More Gratitude Every Day.* Retrieved from Forbes: https://www.forbes.com/sites/womensmedia/2016/07/08/8-ways-to-have-more-gratitude-every-day/?sh=1eebdedf1d54

Miller, J. A. (n.d.). *How to Feed a Runner.* Retrieved 2023, from The New York Times: https://www.nytimes.com/guides/well/healthy-eating-for-runners

Mills, I. J. (2017, August 31). *A person-centred Approach to holistic Assessment*. Retrieved from PubMed: https://pubmed.ncbi.nlm.nih.gov/30188310/

Mindful Living. (n.d.). Retrieved 2023, from mindfulness.com: https://mindfulness.com/mindful-living

Mindful Staff. (2020, July 8). *What is Mindfulness?* Retrieved from mindful.org: https://www.mindful.org/what-is-mindfulness/

Mindful Staff. (2023, April). *How to Meditate*. Retrieved from Mindful: https://www.mindful.org/how-to-meditate/

Mindful Staff. (n.d.). *How to Practice Gratitude*. Retrieved 2023, from mindful.org: https://www.mindful.org/an-introduction-to-mindful-gratitude/

Morin, A. (2015, April 3). *7 Scientifically Proven Benefits of Gratitude*. Retrieved from Psychology Today: https://www.psychologytoday.com/us/blog/what-mentally-strong-people-dont-do/201504/7-scientifically-proven-benefits-of-gratitude

Morris, R. (2021, February 22). *TOP TEN WAYS TO BE A MORE HOLISTIC RUNNER*. Retrieved from Running Planet Journal: https://runningplanetjournal.com/2021/02/22/be-a-more-holistic-runner/

Neitz, K. M. (2014, February 27). *The Whole Body Fix*. Retrieved from Runner's World: https://www.runnersworld.com/health-injuries/a20841319/the-whole-body-fix/

Olivas, M. (n.d.). *Hydration Guide for Runners*. Retrieved 2023, from Run Eat Repeat: https://runeatrepeat.com/hydration-guide-for-runners/

Owens, D., & Brar, F. (2021, October 21). *How I Outran Paralysis to Continue Fundraising for My Son's Illness*. Retrieved from Shape: https://www.shape.com/fitness/training-plans/diane-owens-running-journey-neurofibromatosis-guillain-barre

Parker-Pope, T. (n.d.). *How to Start Running*. Retrieved 2023, from The New York Times: https://www.nytimes.com/guides/well/how-to-start-running

Parry, W. (2013, January 1). *7 Tips to Cultivate Gratitude*. Retrieved from Live Science: https://www.livescience.com/25900-7-tips-gratitude-happiness.html

Peer, M. (2023, January 13). *The Most Powerful Way to Reprogram Your Subconscious Mind To Get*. Retrieved from YouTube.com: https://www.youtube.com/user/marisapeer1

Post Running Recovery Explained – How to Recover From Running The Fast Way. (n.d.). Retrieved 2023, from Runner's Blueprint: https://www.runnersblueprint.com/recovery-for-runners/

Power of Positivity. (2020, February 13). *7 Incredible Studies that Prove the Power of the Mind*. Retrieved from Power of Positivity: https://www.powerofpositivity.com/7-incredible-studies-that-prove-the-power-of-the-mind/

Pratt, M. (2022, February 17). *The Science of Gratitude*. Retrieved from mindful.org: https://www.mindful.org/the-science-of-gratitude/

PsychReel. (2022, January 4). *Tony Robbins DISC Test (Everything you need to know)*. Retrieved from PsychReel: https://psychreel.com/tony-robbins-disc-test/

Quinn, E. M. (2021, June 11). *Why Positive Attitude Is Important in*

Sports. Retrieved from Very Well Fit: https://www.verywellfit.com/attitude-and-sports-performance-3974677

Ragan, T. (2018, June 14). *How to 'overcome' fear* . Retrieved from TEDx Talks: https://www.youtube.com/watch?v=xrWvPo-KaVs

Ramirez, L. (2014, August 11). *Runner's World Performance Nutrition for Runners*. Retrieved from Active: https://www.active.com/running/articles/runner-s-world-performance-nutrition-for-runners

Ramsay, G. C. (2021, August 8). *Eliud Kipchoge is the 'greatest of all time ... in any sport,' says leading performance coach*. Retrieved from CNN: https://www.cnn.com/2021/08/08/sport/eliud-kipchoge-olympic-marathon-spt-intl/index.html

Relationship & Personal Growth Blogs . (2019, January 10). Retrieved from Living Roots Project: https://www.lovingrootsproject.com/allblogposts/tag/mind-body

Resnick, A. C. (2021, September 21). *8 Foods to Eat Before Running*. Retrieved from Byrdie: https://www.byrdie.com/foods-to-eat-before-running-5116538

Richards, K. (2016, August 19). *How Usain Bolt Is An Inspiration For The World On & Off The Track*. Retrieved from Romper: https://www.romper.com/p/how-usain-bolt-is-inspiration-for-the-world-on-off-the-track-16720

Rogers, P. (2021, May 27). *How to Lose Fat and Gain Muscle at the Same Time*. Retrieved from Very Well Fit: https://www.verywellfit.com/mistakes-to-avoid-when-building-muscle-and-losing-fat-3498333

Ross, J. P. (2018, July 31). *4 Expert-Backed Ways to Build Mental Toughness*. Retrieved from Runner's World: https://www.runnersworld.com/runners-stories/a20783068/four-ways-to-build-mental-toughness/

Runner's World. (2021, November 11). *7 Ways to Boost Your Post-Run Recovery.* Retrieved from Runner's World: https://runnersworldonline.com.au/7-ways-post-run-recovery/

Runner's World. (2021, July 7). *How to Build Confidence as a Runner.* Retrieved from Runner's World: https://runnersworldonline.com.au/how-to-build-confidence-as-a-runner/

Runner's World. (2021, February 23). *How to start running today: a beginner's guide* . Retrieved from Runner's World: https://runnersworldonline.com.au/how-to-start-running-today-a-beginners-guide/

Runner's World Editors. (2019, March 23). *10 Things We Learned Reading Meb's Marathon Memoir.* Retrieved from Runner's World: https://www.runnersworld.com/runners-stories/a26895549/26-marathons-meb-keflezighi-book/

Runner's World Editors. (2020, January 23). *What should I eat before a long run?* Retrieved from Runner's World: https://www.runnersworld.com/uk/nutrition/a774073/how-to-fuel-your-long-runs/

Runner's World Editors. (2021, December 10). *Everything You Need to Know About Marathon Training Plans* . Retrieved from Runner's World: https://www.runnersworld.com/training/a19492479/marathon-training-plans/

Runnin' For Sweets. (2020, June 25). *14 Meaningful Running Goal Ideas for Any Runner.* Retrieved from Runnin' For Sweets: https://runninforsweets.com/running-goal-ideas/

Sayer, A. (2022, November 17). *7 Best Supplements For Runners.* Retrieved from Marathon Handbook: https://marathonhandbook.com/7-best-supplements-for-runners/

Schad, T. (2021, July 22). *Is Usain Bolt competing in 2021 Olympics? Jamaican track legend retired in 2017.* Retrieved from USA Today: https://www.usatoday.com/story/sports/olympics/2021/07/21/usain-bolt-retired-what-jamaican-sprinter-doing-after-olympics/7867536002/

Schlichter. (2021, May 14). *The Ultimate Guide to Hydration for Runners.* Retrieved from Nutrition For Running: https://nutritionforrunning.com/the-ultimate-guide-hydration-for-runners/

Scott, E. P. (2020, March 25). *5 Meditation Techniques to Get You Started.* Retrieved from Very Well Mind: https://www.verywellmind.com/different-meditation-techniques-for-relaxation-3144696

Scott, E. P. (2020, July 29). *8 Meditation Techniques to Try.* Retrieved from Very Well Mind: https://www.verywellmind.com/learn-how-to-meditate-3144793

Scott, E. P. (2022, November 16). *How to Deal With FOMO in Your Life.* Retrieved from Very Well Mind: https://www.verywellmind.com/how-to-cope-with-fomo-4174664

Selig, M. (2016, October 28). *8 Things You Didn't Know About Your Mind.* Retrieved from Psychology Today: https://www.psychologytoday.com/us/blog/changepower/201610/8-things-you-didnt-know-about-your-mind

Selva, J. ,. (2017, January 31). *Exploring the Body Mind Connection (Incl. 5 Techniques).* Retrieved from Positive Psychology: https://positivepsychology.com/body-mind-integration-attention-training/

Sommerfeldt, S. C. (2019, July 9). *A HOLISTIC APPROACH TO MIND-BODY WELLNESS.* Retrieved from Living Roots Project: https://www.lovingrootsproject.com/allblogposts/a-holistic-approach-to-mind-body-wellness

St. Michel, C. (2018, October 1). *Mind, Body, Spirit Medicine - A Holistic Approach to Optimal Health.* Retrieved from Cedars Sinai: https://www.cedars-sinai.org/csmagazine/holistic-approach-to-optimal-health.html

Stoerkel, E. M. (2019, February 4). *The Science and Research on Gratitude and Happiness.* Retrieved from Positive Psychology: https://positivepsychology.com/gratitude-happiness-research/

Taylor, J. D. (2017, December 6). *5 Attitudes You Need for Athletic Success 5 Attitudes You Need for Athletic Success Dr. Jim Taylor By Dr. Jim Taylor, Contributor Sport psychologist, parenting expert, professor, author, speaker, elite athlete Apr 5, 2016, 12:36 PM EDT | Updated Dec 6, 2.* Retrieved from Huff Post: https://www.huffpost.com/entry/5-attitudes-you-need-for_b_9618206

Team Tony. (n.d.). *EMPOWERING BELIEFS TO LIVE BY.* Retrieved 2023, from Tony Robbins: https://www.tonyrobbins.com/mind-meaning/empowering-beliefs/

Team Tony. (n.d.). *HOW TO OVERCOME FEAR OF FAILURE.* Retrieved 2023, from Tony Robbins: https://www.tonyrobbins.com/stories/business-mastery/overcoming-fear-failure/

The 8-Week Beginner Running Plan. (n.d.). Retrieved 2023, from Runner's Blueprint: https://www.runnersblueprint.com/beginner-running-plan/

The Athletic Foot Team. (2022, September 1). *A Guide to the Best Vitamins for Runners* . Retrieved from The Athletic Foot: https://theathleticfoot.com/advice/a-guide-to-the-best-vitamins-for-runners/

Thompson, P., & Runners World. (2022, July 28). *How to Run Confidently When You're Just Starting Out.* Retrieved from Runner's World: https://www.runnersworld.com/beginner/a39959355/beginner-tips-for-running-confidently/

Tikkanen, A. (2023, January 16). *Eliud Kipchoge Kenyan distance runner.* Retrieved from Britannica: https://www.britannica.com/biography/Eliud-Kipchoge

Tinsley, G. P. (2018, February 11). *Carb Loading: How to Do It + Common Mistakes*. Retrieved from Healthline: https://www.healthline.com/nutrition/carb-loading

Unlock the power of your mind. (n.d.). Retrieved 2023, from Wim Hof Method: https://www.wimhofmethod.com/power-of-the-mind

Usain Bolt. (n.d.). Retrieved 2023, from Wikipedia: https://en.wikipedia.org/wiki/Usain_Bolt

Usain BOLT. (n.d.). Retrieved 2023, from olympics.com: https://olympics.com/en/athletes/usain-bolt

Usain Bolt's Amazing Life Story and Sayings. (n.d.). Retrieved 2023, from Inspirational Stories: https://www.inspirationalstories.com/usain-bolt-story-and-sayings/

Van Allen, J. (2022, November 23). *Tips on How to Start Running Again So You Make the Ultimate Comeback.* Retrieved from Runner's World: https://www.runnersworld.com/beginner/

Van De Walle, G. M. (2018, October 16). *What to Eat Before Running.* Retrieved from Healthline: https://www.healthline.com/nutrition/what-to-eat-before-running

Waehner, P. (2022, October 5). *How to Use the FITT Principle for Efficient Workouts*. Retrieved from Very Well Fit: https://www.verywellfit.com/f-i-t-t-principle-what-you-need-for-great-workouts-1231593

Walsh, K. (2023, February 22). *The Best Diets for Runners, According to*

Dietitians. Retrieved from Runner's World: https://www.runnersworld.co.za/nutrition/the-best-diets-for-runners-according-to-dietitians/

WebMD Editorial Contributors. (2021, October 25). *What is Mindfulness Meditation?* Retrieved from Web MD: https://www.webmd.com/balance/what-is-mindfulness-meditation

White, P. G. (n.d.). *Beginners Guide to Meditation*. Retrieved 2023, from Mindworks: https://mindworks.org/blog/beginners-guide-meditation/

Why You Should Run A Gratitude Mile. (2020, May 1). Retrieved from Runner's World: https://www.pressreader.com/uk/runners-world-uk/20200501/281500753352337

Wierzbicka, A., Pedersen, E., Persson, R., & Nordquist, B. (2018, August). *Healthy Indoor Environments: The Need for a Holistic Approach*. Retrieved from Research Gate: https://www.researchgate.net/publication/327336264_Healthy_Indoor_Environments_The_Need_for_a_Holistic_Approach

Zubricky, R. (2021, January 15). *The Holistic Approach to Running*. Retrieved from Illinois Marathon: https://illinoismarathon.com/the-holistic-approach-to-running/

Made in the USA
Middletown, DE
21 May 2023